# A STORY OF SHALOM

*The Calling of Christians and Jews
by a Covenanting God*

# Studies in Judaism and Christianity

*Exploration of Issues in the Contemporary Dialogue Between Christians and Jews*

Editor in Chief for
Stimulus Books
Helga Croner

Editors
Lawrence Boadt, C.S.P.
Helga Croner
Rabbi Leon Klenicki
Kevin A. Lynch, C.S.P.
Dennis McManus

A STIMULUS BOOK

# A STORY OF SHALOM

*The Calling of Christians and Jews
by a Covenanting God*

**Philip A. Cunningham**

**A STIMULUS BOOK**

**PAULIST PRESS ◆ NEW YORK ◆ MAHWAH, N.J.**

*Cover design by A. Michael Velthaus*

Library of Congress Cataloging-in-Publication Data

Cunningham, Philip A.
    A story of shalom  :  the calling of Christians and Jews by a covenanting God / by Philip A. Cunningham.
        p.   cm.—(Stimulus series)
    Includes bibliographical references and index.
    ISBN 0-8091-4014-4 (alk. paper)
    1. Church history. 2. Christianity and other religions—Judaism. 3. Judaism—Relations—Chistianity.    4. Theology, Doctrinal—Comparative  studies.    5. Judaism—Doctrines—Comparative studies. I. Title. II. Series.
BR145.2 .C86  2001
231.7′6—dc21

                                                                2001021024

Published by Paulist Press
997 Macarthur Boulevard
Mahwah, New Jersey 07430

www.paulistpress.com

Printed and bound in the
United States of America

# Contents

## Acknowledgments

This book was written in two distinct phases. I would like to convey my gratitude to Notre Dame College of Manchester, New Hampshire, for granting me a sabbatical in the spring of 1998, which enabled me to do most of its research and first drafting. The participants in the June 1998 "Ministry Foundations Program" and in the "Church Through the Ages" course in the fall semester of 1998 offered beneficial remarks during these early drafting stages—thank you, all! Special appreciation is due to Dr. Barbara Anne Radtke for her insightful theological comments and questions and to Dr. Charles Lasher for his historical review. The second writing stage occurred during the initial development of the new Center for Christian-Jewish Learning at Boston College. I am most indebted to Dr. Eugene Fisher, Dr. Paula Fredriksen, and Rabbi Dr. Ruth Langer for their very helpful insights and opinions. Obviously, I am responsible for any errors or oversights in the finished product. Lastly, I must gratefully express my love to my wife, Julia Anne Walsh, and my children, Francis and Diana, for their support and patience as this project unfolded.

*Dedicated to*

*Francis and Diana*

May the century in which you will be adults see
the maturation of true *shalom* between Christians and Jews.

# Abbreviations of Church Documents Cited

## Document Collections

| *Abbreviation* | *Document or Document Collection* |
|---|---|
| CDF, *Dominus Iesus* (2000). | Congregation for the Doctrine of the Faith*, Dominus Iesus*: *Declaration on the Unicity and Salvific Universality of Jesus Christ and the Church* (August 6, 2000). http://www.vatican.va/roman_ curia/congregations/cfaith/ documents/rc_con_cfaith_doc_20000 806_dominus-iesus_en.html |
| Croner, *Stepping Stones*. | Helga Croner, ed., *Stepping Stones to Further Jewish-Christian Relations* (London/New York: Stimulus Books, 1977). |
| Croner, *More Stepping Stones*. | Helga Croner, ed*., More Stepping Stones to Jewish-Christian Relations: An Unabridged Collection of Christian Documents, 1975–1983* (New York/ Mahwah, N.J.: Paulist Press/Stimulus Books, 1985). |
| Fisher and Klenicki, *Spiritual Pilgrimage.* | Eugene J. Fisher and Leon Klenicki, eds., *Spiritual Pilgrimage: Pope John* |

|  | *Paul II, Texts on Jews and Judaism 1979–1995* (New York: Crossroad, 1995). |
|---|---|
| Vatican Council II, *[document name]*. | Austin Flannery, gen. ed., *Vatican Council II: Constitutions, Decrees, Declarations* (Northport, N.Y./Dublin, Ireland: Costello Publishing/Dominican Publications, 1996). |
| WCC, *Churches and Jewish People*. | World Council of Churches, *The Theology of the Churches and the Jewish People: Statements by the World Council of Churches and Its Member Churches* (Geneva: W.C.C. Publications, 1988). |

## Individual Documents

| *CCC* (1994). | *Catechism of the Catholic Church* (Washington, D.C.: U.S.C.C., 1994). |
|---|---|
| John Paul II, "Address to the Jewish Community —West Germany" (Nov. 17, 1980). | "Address to the Jewish Community—West Germany" (Nov. 17, 1980), in Fisher and Klenicki, *Spiritual Pilgrimage,* pp. 13–16. |
| John Paul II, "Address to Jewish Leaders in Miami" (Sept 11, 1987). | John Paul II, "Address to Jewish Leaders in Miami" (Sept. 11, 1987), in Fisher and Klenicki, *Spiritual Pilgrimage,* pp. 105–9. |
| John Paul II, "Address to Jewish Leaders in Warsaw" (June 14, 1987). | John Paul II, "Address to Jewish Leaders in Warsaw," June 14, 1987, in Fisher and Klenicki, *Spiritual Pilgrimage,* pp. 98–99. |
| John Paul II, "Evolution" (1996). | John Paul II, "Message to the Pontifical Academy of Sciences on Evolution" (October 22, 1996), 4 in *Origins* 26/25 (December 5, 1996): 414–16. |

| | |
|---|---|
| John Paul II, *Fides et Ratio* (1998). | John Paul II, *Fides et Ratio* in *Origins* 28/19 (October 22, 1998): 317–48. |
| John Paul II, "Galileo" (1992). | John Paul II, "Address to the Pontifical Academy of Sciences" (October 31, 1992) in *Origins* 22/22 (November 12, 1992): 369–74. |
| John Paul II, "PBC Address" (1997). | John Paul II, "Address to the Pontifical Biblical Commission," *L'Osservatore Romano,* April 23, 1997, p. 2. |
| John Paul II, *Tertio Millennio Adveniente* (1994). | John Paul II, *Tertio Millennio Adveniente* in *Origins* 24/24 (November 24, 1994): 401–16. |
| NCCB, *Economic Justice* (1986). | National Conference of Catholic Bishops, *Economic Justice for All* (Washington, D.C.: U.S.C.C., 1986). |
| NCCB, *God's Mercy* (1988). | Bishops' Committee on the Liturgy, National Conference of Catholic Bishops, *God's Mercy Endures Forever: Guidelines on the Presentation of Jews and Judaism in Catholic Preaching* (Washington, D.C.: U.S.C.C., 1988). |
| NCCB, "Statement" (1975). | National Conference of Catholic Bishops, Washington, D.C., "Statement on Jewish Christian Relations" (1975), in Croner, *Stepping Stones,* 29–34. |
| NCCB et al., *Within Context* (1987). | Secretariat for Catholic-Jewish Relations, N.C.C.B.; Adult Education Dept., U.S.C.C.; Interfaith Affairs Dept., ADL, *Within Context: Guidelines for the Catechetical Presentation of Jews and Judaism in the New Testament* (Morristown, N.J.: Silver Burdett and Ginn, 1987). |

PBC, "Bible and Christology" (1984).

Pontifical Biblical Commission, "Instruction on the Bible and Christology," in Joseph A. Fitzmyer, *Scripture and Christology* (New York/Mahwah, N.J.: Paulist Press, 1986).

PBC, "Gospels" (1964).

Pontifical Biblical Commission, "Instruction on the Historical Truth of the Gospels" excerpted in Raymond E. Brown, *Biblical Reflections on Crises Facing the Church* (New York/Paramus, N.J.: Paulist Press, 1975), pp. 111–15.

PBC, "Interpretation" (1993).

Pontifical Biblical Commission, "The Interpretation of the Bible in the Church," (1993) in *Origins* 23/29 (January 6, 1994): 499–524.

Vatican, "Ecumenism" (1993).

Pontifical Council for Promoting Christian Unity, "Directory for the Application of Principles and Norms on Ecumenism," in *Origins* 23/9 (July 29, 1993): 129–60.

Vatican, "Guidelines" (1974).

Vatican Commission for Religious Relations with the Jews, "Guidelines and Suggestions for Implementing the Conciliar Declaration *Nostra Aetate,* No. 4" (1974), in Croner, *Stepping Stones,* pp. 11–16.

Vatican, "Notes" (1985).

Vatican Commission for Religious Relations with the Jews, "Notes on the Correct Way to Present Jews and Judaism in Preaching and Catechesis in the Roman Catholic Church" (1985), II, 7, in *Origins* 15/7 (July 4, 1985): 102–7.

Vatican, *We Remember* (1998).

Vatican Commission for Religious Relations with the Jews, *We Remember: A Reflection on the Shoah* (Vatican City: Typis Vaticanis, 1998).

WCC, "The Church and the Jewish People" (1967).

The Commission on Faith and Order, The World Council of Churches, "The Church and the Jewish People" V (1967), in W.C.C., *Churches and Jewish People,* pp. 13–28.

WCC, "Ecumenical Considerations" (1982).

The Executive Committee of the World Council of Churches, "Ecumenical Considerations on Jewish-Christian Dialogue" (July 16, 1982), in W.C.C., *Churches and Jewish People,* pp. 34–42.

[West] German Bishops' Conference, "The Church and the Jews" (1980).

[West] German Bishops' Conference, "The Church and the Jews" (1980), in Croner, *More Stepping Stones,* pp. 124–45.

# Prelude: Why Tell the Christian Story in a New Way?

This book is an experiment. It is an effort to retell the Christian story in an unprecedented situation at the dawn of the third millennium of the church's existence. In the aftermath of the *Shoah,* most Christian denominations have begun to think seriously about a topic little considered since the days of the Apostle Paul. This topic, which Paul describes in Romans 11:25 as a mystery, is the relationship between the Jewish and Christian peoples. The recent reexamination of this relationship has major implications for Christian self-definition and teachings. As a Roman Catholic, I will approach these topics from within my own faith-community and I will often cite its teaching documents. Nonetheless, I believe that my basic points are relevant to the vast majority of Christian churches.

What do I mean by "the Christian story"? It is a master narrative that expresses what Christianity is all about. It tells about God, Jesus Christ, and salvation. It speaks about the origins of the church, its purposes, its doings over the centuries, and its goals for the future. Most Christians have some such sweeping tale either consciously or unconsciously embedded in their religious imaginations. It helps them interpret new experiences that the church and its members encounter. These experiences, in turn, can revise or refine aspects of the Christian story.

A certain telling of the foundational Christian story has prevailed for almost twenty centuries. I would outline this "classic" story as follows:[1]

## THE CLASSIC FOUNDATIONAL CHRISTIAN STORY

1. God created the world and created humanity in the divine image.
2. God wanted humanity to live in happiness with God.
3. Humanity sinned through disobedience. They were driven from God's presence into a world of toil, disease, and death.
4. God promised to send a savior. The people of Israel prepared for his coming.
5. Eventually, the Son of God was incarnated as a human, and died for the sins of humanity.
6. Through baptism into Christ, people can now become united with God. If they live Christian lives, they will spend eternity with God in heaven.
7. One day this world will end and God's Kingdom will prevail.

I submit that this classic story line needs revising for use in today's church. Several factors demand that the Christian religious imagination of the third millennium be shaped in different ways than previously.

*1. We No Longer Think We Have Replaced Jews as God's Chosen People*

In the second through fourth centuries of the Common Era, two forces motivated Christian apologists to develop an anti-Jewish theology: (1) pagan criticisms of the church as a heretical deviation from Judaism; and (2) the immense attractiveness of Judaism for both Christians and non-Christians in the Roman Empire.[2] Following the rhetorical customs of the time, church leaders in this patristic era drew upon polemical passages in the

Christian Testament[3] to enhance Christianity's status by denigrating its Jewish rival. In a body of literature known as the *adversus Judaeos* tradition, but also in commentaries, sermons, and Christian instructions, originally disparate claims were organized into an anti-Jewish theological superstructure. It was premised upon the conviction that the church had superseded Judaism as God's chosen people because of the Jewish rejection and killing of Christ. "The Fathers of the Church of the first centuries, as much in the East as in the West, were in agreement in showing the Jewish people as 'repudiated' definitively by God, and the Church as the selected people in 'substitution' to bring salvation to everyone."[4] This "supersessionism" was well expressed in these words of the third-century theologian Origen:

> One of the facts that show that Jesus was some divine and holy person is just that on his account such great and fearful disasters have now for a long time befallen the Jews....For they committed the most impious crime of all, when they plotted against the Savior of mankind, in the city where they performed to God the customary rites that were symbols of profound mysteries. Therefore that city where Jesus suffered these humiliations had to be utterly destroyed. The Jewish nation had to be overthrown, and God's invitation to blessedness yielded to others, I mean the Christians, to whom came the teaching about the simple and pure worship of God. And they received new laws that fit in with the order established everywhere.[5]

This supersessionist understanding dominated Christian thinking for over a millennium. It contributed to what the U.S. Catholic Bishops have called "a de-Judaizing process" in Christianity. It led "not only to social friction with the Jews but often to their oppression."[6] In the words of Cardinal Edward Idris Cassidy, President of the Vatican Commission for Religious Relations with the Jews, the "anti-Jewish tradition stamped its mark in different ways on Christian doctrine and teaching."[7]

To put it another way, supersessionism stamped its mark on how the Christian story has been told. The "classic" account outlined above is premised on supersessionism. In it Israel existed only to prepare for the redemptive act of Christ and once that was accomplished Israel really had little reason to continue to exist. It had been rendered obsolete.

An unrevised classic story cannot be told today in a church that has renounced supersessionism. This is a new moment in Christian history. In the decades since the *Shoah,* church instructions across a wide range of denominations have officially repudiated two cornerstones of supersessionism. These documents declare that the Jewish people remain in a perpetual covenantal relationship with God and condemn any blaming of "the Jews" for the crucifixion of Jesus.[8] As Pope John Paul II has stated on numerous occasions, Jews are "the people of God of the Old Covenant, never revoked by God";[9] "the present-day people of the Covenant concluded with Moses";[10] and partners "in a covenant of eternal love which was never revoked."[11] Today's church is postsupersessionist. It rejects supersessionism.

Many of these documents also understand that Judaism has an ongoing vocation in the world that Christians must learn to accept in terms of Jewish self-understanding.[12] In addition, due to its historic origins, the Christian story cannot be told without reference to Judaism. As the Catholic bishops of West Germany expressed it, "He who encounters Jesus Christ encounters Judaism."[13] Thus whenever today's postsupersessionist church tells its story anew, it inevitably must affirm the validity of Jewish self-understandings of Israel's covenantal life with God.

Moreover, as the Commission on Faith and Order of the World Council of Churches noted, "there is no doctrine of Christian theology which is not influenced in some way by the confrontation with the Jewish people."[14] Therefore, an acknowledgment of Israel's ongoing covenant will automatically impact many theological disciplines, including christology, ecclesiology, and soteriology. Today's postsupersessionist Christian story will necessarily have to speak differently about Jesus, the church, and salvation than did the supersessionist classic rendition because "the entire self-understanding of the Church is at stake."[15]

## 2. *We Now Read the Bible Differently Than Previous Generations*

In the twentieth century, historical and literary critical methods of reading the Bible spread throughout many Christian denominations. Such approaches recognize that the cultures, traditions, literary conventions, and circumstances of the writers of the Bible have shaped the compositions of their texts. Therefore, these influences must be historically reconstructed when seeking the intended meanings of their words. In my own Roman Catholic community:

> The historical-critical method is the indispensable method for the scientific study of the meaning of ancient texts. Holy Scripture, inasmuch as it is the "word of God in human language," has been composed by human authors in all its various parts and in all the sources that lie behind them. Because of this, its proper understanding not only admits the use of this method but actually requires it....[O]ne must reject as inauthentic every interpretation alien to the meaning expressed by the human authors in their written text.[16]

The last sentence also means that the intentions of the biblical writers now serve as a template for judging the appropriateness of later applications of them in Christian history. This is particularly significant for the texts of the Shared Testament,[17] which have traditionally been read in the church only as foreshadowings of Christianity.

The principles of biblical historical-criticism and concern for Jewish-Christian relations have combined in an instruction to Catholic preachers "to avoid approaches that reduce [the "Old" Testament] to a propaedeutic or background for the New

Testament."[18] This, of course, is precisely what was done when supersessionism prevailed and molded the classic telling of the Christian story.

This point can be illustrated by considering God's words to the serpent in Genesis 3:15: "I will put enmity between you and the woman, and between your offspring and hers; he will strike your head, and you will strike his heel." Some versions of the supersessionist classic Christian story claimed that those words constituted a divine promise "to send into the world a Savior to free man from his sins and to reopen to him the gates of heaven."[19] Thus, at the very beginning of Israel's scriptures, Israel was introduced as merely a preparation for Christianity.

Historical-critical exegeses of this Genesis passage typically see no such meaning intended by its Yahwistic author. "Christian tradition has sometimes referred to [the offspring] as Christ, but the literal reference is to the human descendants of Eve, who will regard snakes as enemies."[20] If Catholics today "must reject as inauthentic every interpretation alien to the meaning expressed by the human authors in their written text,"[21] then Christian stories based on what are now identified as eisegetical readings of biblical texts cannot be told without significant qualification. The sacred writers' intentions would need to be honored first before noting subsequent interpretations in the church's history.

Historical criticism also diminishes the authority and influence of polemical scriptural passages. For example, statements about Jews, such as John 8:44, "You are from your father the devil" or Matthew 27:25, "His blood be on us and our children!" are critically understood as products of their authors' specific contentious situations.[22] They therefore do not have normative value for the entire Christian tradition for all time.

Not only are Catholics instructed to read the Bible critically, we are also admonished not to actualize or apply in our contemporary context any understandings of scripture that demean Jews and Judaism. In the words of the Pontifical Biblical Commission:

> Particular attention is necessary, according to the spirit of
> the Second Vatican Council (*Nostra Aetate,* 4), to avoid
> absolutely any actualization of certain texts of the New
> Testament which could provoke or reinforce unfavorable
> attitudes toward the Jewish people. The tragic events of the
> past must, on the contrary, impel all to keep unceasingly in
> mind that, according to the New Testament, the Jews remain
> "beloved" of God, "since the gifts and calling of God are
> irrevocable" (Rom 11:28–29).[23]

Present-day retellings of the Christian story, since they must
be significantly based on the biblical witness, in fact involve the
actualizations of the scriptures for our times. Again, the story cannot be told in ways that promote "unfavorable attitudes toward
the Jewish people."

In sum, the rise of historical-critical biblical methodologies
provides additional reasons why the classic version of the
Christian story must be revised.

## 3.  Our Way of Discerning Reality Is Different from That of Earlier Christians

A historical consciousness pervades Western society in our
post-Freudian, post-Darwinian, post-Mendelian era. This is an
awareness that people's experiences, cultures, and histories mold
their subjective consciousness and perceptions. It grounds biblical historical-criticism as just discussed. This mindfulness of cultural conditioning also relates to our current societal preferences
for an experience-based approach to reality and for empirically
demonstrable truth claims.

However, the classic Christian story is significantly based
on certain Greek philosophies that were the prevalent mode of
thought in the patristic era when many Christian doctrines were
formulated. Major concepts underlying the Christian story were
established in an intellectual environment that was concerned

with rationally defining the inherent *ontos* of God and reality. These were philosophies based on an ontological metaphysics that sought to deduce rationally the essential being of transcendent realities.

"Metaphysical theology," explains Joseph Stephen O'Leary, "wants to construct an account of Christ independent of faith and of historical context, an account which can be indifferently repeated in any historical context."[24] It supposes that people can step outside history through reason. This is a notion that conflicts with current Western culture's acute awareness of the historical and cultural conditioning of personal perceptions.[25]

This is one reason why certain elements of the classic rendition of the Christian story sound alien to believers today and require intense explanation. As O'Leary notes:

> Within the horizons of [ontology] Nicea and Chalcedon said all that could be said, and needed to be said, about Christ. Yet for us the question about Christ and its answer can no longer be formulated in that particular way. The question, "Who do you say that I am?" (Mark 8:29) continues to sound in a pre-metaphysical way, but the metaphysical tradition is of only indirect assistance to us in our search for a contemporary answer.[26]

This leads me to a pastoral and educational decision: the Christian story told today should not be articulated according to currently unfamiliar philosophical presuppositions, but rather should utilize the prevalent historical consciousness.[27] It must be stressed that an avoidance of ontological metaphysics and an employment of historically conscious ideas do not equal a denial of the existence of the Transcendent. It simply means that the Transcendent can only be discerned and rationally considered by mortals as it is mediated in the created world through history. This is true even when the Transcendent discloses itself in revelation because revelation is encountered in historical experiences. As Pope John Paul II has put it, "History...becomes the arena where we see what God does for humanity. God comes to us in the things we know best and can verify most easily, the things of our everyday life, apart from which we cannot understand ourselves."[28]

Nor is this move a rejection of the spiritual wealth of patristic philosophical theologizing. The labors of the church fathers produced a rich apprehension of the divine realities that should be honored and preserved in the Christian tradition. But people possessing a historical consciousness must discern and articulate these realities in historically conscious ways.[29]

However, this leads to another reason to avoid patristic-era metaphysical approaches in relating postsupersessionist versions of the Christian story. Jewish understandings of God often conflict with rational, ontological outlooks. As Bernard J. Lee explains:

> We exist in the world in our bodies. We exist in the world in time. We can only know what is related to us in the world and is together with us in time. To claim to experience God is also, therefore, to claim that God is in the world with us, and that God, therefore, is truly historical. In classical theism, the religious object (God) is not historical. God is interpreted as essentially nontemporal. The biblical experience witnesses to the contrary: God is an essential component of the evolving history of the Jewish people. But equally, Jewish history is a real component of the experience of God, which is to say, of the concrete reality of God.[30]

The historically necessary patristic engagement with a particular type of metaphysical theologizing was thus also a move away from the relational view of life characteristic of the Hebrew/Jewish biblical tradition. This philosophical step occurred in the same era when socio-religious rivalry was spurring the creation of the *adversus Judaeos* theology. The patristic philosophical milieu and its competitive social setting thus concurrently reinforced the gradual process of de-Judaizing Christianity that was mentioned by the U.S. Catholic Bishops.[31]

Conversely, an effort to tell the Christian story non-ontolog-ically could contribute to a renewed appreciation of the church's Jewish roots and of its kinship with Judaism today. As O'Leary observes, "The step back out of [ontological] metaphysical theol-ogy is a step towards the Jewish matrix of all our theology....It is thus perhaps in the renewal of Jewish-Christian dialogue that the counter-metaphysical protest of the last four or five centuries is carried forward most radically today."[32]

Given this decision to avoid certain metaphysical approaches, and given the historical consciousness that characterizes Western society, I will proceed in retelling the Christian story with the following premise. Since we are human beings immersed in and restricted by time and space, our knowledge of God, the Transcendent One beyond time or space, is limited to how we sen-sibly experience God in our lives, histories, rituals, and traditions. Even though God may be powerfully and truly encountered, our knowledge of God is invariably partial and always mediated.[33] Faith communities' knowledge of God grows and becomes norma-tive as their traditions unfold, but such knowledge is always open to further growth and to being experienced anew.

Thus, in the ensuing story, the Trinity will not be described ontologically. Rather, the triune God will be portrayed as relation-ally experienced, as constantly and simultaneously creating and sustaining, inviting into relationship, and empowering that invita-tion's acceptance. Likewise, Jesus Christ will not be described ontologically in terms of a hypostatic union of two natures, but as the Christian experience of the Raised Crucified One who medi-ates relationship with God. This move is not a denial of the truths that were expressed of old in ontological ways. Nor does it reject "metaphysics," in the sense of denying transhistorical reality. Instead, a "metaphysics of relationship" will ground this rendi-tion of the Christian story.[34] This might also be expressed as a "relational ontology."[35]

## 4. We Now Think in Terms of Processes of Development

Evolutionary science is a fourth reason for recrafting the Christian story. Although opposed to evolutionary principles for over a century, those Christian denominations that have advocated biblical criticism now see no opposition between them and Christian faith. To cite again my own Roman Catholic community as an example, Pope John Paul II told the Pontifical Academy of Sciences:

> [N]ew knowledge leads to the recognition of the theory of evolution as more than a hypothesis. It is indeed remarkable that this theory has been progressively accepted by researchers following a series of discoveries in various fields of knowledge. The convergence, neither sought nor provoked, of the results of work that was conducted independently is itself a significant argument in favor of this theory.[36]

Ecclesial recognition of the overwhelming scientific evidence in support of evolutionary processes will affect how the Christian story recounts creation and the origins of humanity. According to John Haught, "evolution has made theology see that the universe could not logically have been created complete and perfected in one instant. It only follows, then, that we live in an unfinished universe. But an unfinished universe, by definition, is imperfect, however much it may be on the road to perfection."[37] This perspective happens to accord quite well with Jewish interpretations of Genesis 1, which tend to see God fashioning an incomplete world so that humanity can creatively participate in its completion.[38]

In addition, an evolutionary viewpoint influences how death is explained and therefore also affects how salvation is to be understood. Evolutionary perspectives call into question Christian interpretations of Genesis 2 and 3 that draw the *historical* and ontological conclusion that death was a punishment for the disobedience of Adam and Eve (so suggested by Rom 5:12

and 6:23) and that it was the result of a fall from a previous death-less existence. There are good exegetical reasons for doubting whether the Yahwist was thinking in such terms,[39] but the point here is that an acceptance of evolutionary processes in principle disallows unexamined claims that earthly life, especially human life, was ever deathless and therefore that death is a punishment.[40]

That this is an unresolved tension in present Catholic teach-ing can be seen, I think, in the 1994 *Catechism of the Catholic Church.* It states that "[t]he account of the fall in Genesis 3 uses figurative language, but affirms a primeval event, a deed that took place *at the beginning of the history of man.*"[41] How an admittedly "figurative" account can be understood as pointing to a single, historical "primeval event," which given an evolutionary outlook must have occurred thousands or even millions of years before the Yahwist wrote this narrative, is not explained. Likewise the sentence that "Even though man's nature is mortal, God had des-tined him not to die"[42] is confusing, if not contradictory. The word *nature* is a cue that this is an ontologically driven reading of the scriptures, rather than an exegetical or an evolutionary-conscious one. The unavoidable conclusion seems to be that an acceptance of current evolutionary viewpoints means that present-day itera-tions of the Christian story are necessarily going to differ signifi-cantly from pre-Darwinian versions.

This retelling of the Christian story, influenced as it is by scientific evolutionary perspectives, is not based on the conven-tional notion of an ontological "fall" from deathlessness to mor-tality. However, the Christian concept of "original sin" certainly does appear in these pages, although it is described socially and behaviorally rather than ontologically. Humanity is portrayed as all too eager to exercise its capacity to make moral choices in destructive, sinful ways. The persistent social allure to make sin-ful decisions is seen as pervading human cultures and so infecting successive generations of humanity.

In line with this, this narration of the Christian story will emphasize how this sinful situation conflicts with divine intentions for humanity. Far from assisting God in bringing creation to its fulfillment, social inducements to egotism and self-aggrandizement inhibit humanity from fulfilling its intended creative role. Hence, salvation will be understood as people being sustained, invited, and enabled by the Triune One to move toward a rejection of sinful behaviors in order to participate covenantally in God's unfolding designs for humanity and for the created universe.

## 5. *We Should Tell the Christian Story So As to Promote Shalom*

To summarize, retellings of the Christian story today must: (1) affirm Judaism's covenanting with God and the validity of Jewish self-understanding; (2) incorporate critical methods for interpreting the scriptures; (3) operate with a contemporary historical consciousness and avoid ahistorical ontological approaches; and (4) respect current scientific insights. To be an *effective* story, it must also define, enable, and foster Christian discipleship.

What follows, then, is a retelling of the Christian story according to these criteria. I have chosen to offer this experiment in articulating a postsupersessionist theology through the genre of a narrative for several reasons. Although tremendous progress has been made in recent decades in removing the negative Christian teaching of contempt for Jews and Judaism from official statements and textbooks,[43] there has not been sufficient time to reshape similarly the popular Christian religious imagination. My experience in working with parish ministers and church groups is that Catholic teaching about the intrinsic kinship between Christians and Jews[44] has not yet been internalized to the point that it shapes our prayer and self-definitions. However, narratives or stories have a power to shape people's religious imaginations and identities that exceeds technical exposition or formal lessons. This is probably because of a story's ability to use ordinary speech to convey multiple and tensive layers of meanings. My own background in biblical studies and religious education is an influence here as well. I hope that this effort will prove to be interesting and meaningful and thought-provoking to as many readers as possible. While I recognize that this project has wide implications in many branches of theology and must draw upon many additional disciplines, I have chosen to favor a sweeping conciseness over exhaustive analysis. Hopefully, this small experiment will stimulate other similar efforts so that the Christian story can be told with candor and vigor and effectiveness in the new millennium.

This story is a narrative theology with significant historical content. It is not claimed that the historical elements are presented in an imaginary, purely "objective" fashion. Instead, the story intentionally conveys a history *interpreted* through the lens of Christian faith in general and Roman Catholic perspectives in particular. The facts that this version of the Christian story is told by a middle-aged male Irish Roman Catholic, a member of a Western Christian denomination, citizen of the United States, and college professor should also be kept in mind. Other tellers of the tale will offer different and enriching renditions of the story. Again, I hope this endeavor might prompt other Christians to tell their stories in ways that likewise are affirming of the ongoing covenanting between God and the people of Israel.

Since one of my intentions is to suggest ways of reconfiguring the Christian religious imagination and its grasp of the church's purposes, the text is written for nonspecialists as well as for those with theological expertise. Roman Catholics will especially relate to the references to our community's teaching documents, but members of other Christian denominations will, I hope, find these materials helpful since all Christians must wrestle with these same issues. Jewish readers will, of course, be in the role of interested observers to a process of faith expression that is essentially a Christian task. However, they have an invaluable role to play by assessing whether Christian reflections and descriptions of the Jewish tradition are fair and accurate.

As was true of earlier versions of the Christian story, this version begins with God's creation of the existing universe.

Reflecting our developing knowledge of cosmology and of the processes of evolution, its opening and closing sections will hopefully encourage a certain humility by stressing the smallness of humanity amidst the vastness of the universe. In addition, while recognizing the positive achievements of Christianity, this broad summary of the church's history will also acknowledge the serious failures of Christians down through the ages. This is in keeping with the recent words of Pope John Paul II:

> It is appropriate that, as the Second Millennium of Christianity draws to a close, the Church should become more fully conscious of the sinfulness of her children, recalling those times in history when they departed from the spirit of Christ and his Gospel and, instead of offering to the world the witness of a life inspired by the values of faith, indulged in ways of thinking and acting which were truly forms of counter-witness and scandal.[45]

After summarizing Christian history, this story's ending will bring us to the present moment and our responsibility as Christians toward the final destiny of things, when "God will be all in all" (1 Cor 15:28).

Throughout this historical-theological narrative, endnotes will point to pertinent Catholic documents and to the work of certain theologians for particular ideas taken up within the story. Rather than unnecessarily cluttering the notes with the sources used for general historical information, the list of works consulted that follows the story will acknowledge the contributions made by various scholars to the overall sweep of the telling of this story.

Finally, a word should be offered about the title of this work. This is the fourth volume in which I have included the Hebrew word *shalom* in the title.[46] This is because I find the many connotations of this word to be particularly relevant to the relationship between Judaism and Christianity. Usually translated into English as peace, *shalom* actually denotes prosperity, ease, well-being, and a sense of being whole and healthy. It is associated with being in right relationship within one's own community and with others. *Shalom* is also sometimes understood as the fruit of God's salvation.

It seems certain that Christianity has not been in "right relationship" with Judaism throughout most of the two millennia of its existence. Cardinal Edward Cassidy has summarized this history in these words:

> There can be no denial of the fact that from the time of the Emperor Constantine on, Jews were isolated and discriminated against in the Christian world. There were expulsions and forced conversions. Literature propagated stereotypes, preaching accused the Jews of every age of deicide; the ghetto which came into being in 1555 with a papal bull became in Nazi Germany the antechamber of the extermination....The church can justly be accused of not showing to the Jewish people down through the centuries that love which its founder, Jesus Christ, made the fundamental principle of its teaching.[47]

Given this tragic assessment, one ponders to what extent the church's lack of *shalom* with Judaism has impeded its continuation of the mission of Jesus to prepare the world for the Reign of God. If over the centuries the Christian community has not been in right relationship with its Jewish roots, indeed in some ways with its Jewish Lord, then how successful could it be in being an agent of *shalom* in the world?

The Catholic Church, together with most other Christian denominations, begins its third millennium having renounced its supersessionist past. The church cultivates *shalom* with "the People of the Covenant"[48] to the extent that it accomplishes its ongoing reform of the legacy of supersessionism. Such shalom brings both external "right relationship" with the Jewish people and internal "right relationship" between the church's Jewish heritage and its unique identity in Christ. This wholeness seems essential if either Jews or Christians are to fulfill their covenanting responsibilities before God toward the rest of humanity.

# A Story of Shalom

This is a story about the Christian people. It does not relate everything that could be told about us, nor does it reckon with the stories of all the other peoples whose journeys ultimately will become wrapped up with ours. It does, however, speak much about the people of Israel, because our story cannot be told without reference to theirs. It is also an unfinished story. Nonetheless, as the third millennium of Christianity begins, this story highlights our past, our present, and the mission for the future in which we Christians are engaged.

*1. Creation*

Before the beginning—God!

Utterly creative, utterly relational, utterly empowering, this One brought forth and sustains time, space, matter, and energy and the diverse forces that interact among them. In their first moments of existence, these all collide and transform. They expand toward intended goals—increasing complexity and the birthing of life and of minds capable of the awareness, love, and creativity that allows relationship with the One and generates lives similarly grounded in creative, empowering relationship.

Being beyond created time, this One would take time barely conceivable by later humans to shape existence's unfolding purposes. Random chance is divinely willed to be inherent in the functioning of this emerging universe down to the quantum level. The universe thus has an unpredictable quality for all those immersed within time's flow. Quarks, atoms, molecules, quasars, galaxies, stars explode and crash, fashioning heavier elements and compounds, gradually forming basic molecules of life. Worlds beyond number, environments beyond imagining, life in incomprehensible varieties—all are produced by the boundless inventiveness of the One.

This story concerns just one little world among the infinity of worlds that God has set spinning through the void. It is situated out toward the edge of a group of hundreds of billions of stars, far away from the cataclysmic ravages of the black hole at that galaxy's center.

In the course of time it comes to teem with ever-changing life. Life and death, destruction and renewal are woven into the One's developing designs. The shifting shapes of its continents, explosive impacts from comets and meteorites, ice ages marching across its surface, mass extinctions of species—all are taken up into the designs of the One. And for One beyond time nothing is ever truly lost.


## 2. Humanity

In the depths of time, sentient creatures gradually appear on this small globe. Through processes empowered by the divine will for relationship, humanity is slowly and carefully called into being. Of all the living things on this verdant world, they share the divine spark in a unique way.[49] They grow into reflective self-awareness. They devise tools that advance their physical abilities to manipulate their environment. They begin to communicate through the instrument of symbolic language. These actions encourage further development of their brain structures. They emerge as inherently social beings, craving relationship with one another.[50] As they spread across the globe, different populations of humans become isolated from one another because of geographic and climatic changes. They acquire distinctive traits as they adapt to changing environments. The image of the One who called them forth is reflected equally amid a wonderful human diversity.

As their consciousness increases, they become aware of their own mortality, their own limitations. They perceive that they live in a world paradoxically imbued with both randomness and order.

In retrospect, one of the greatest gifts of the One to humans eventually becomes evident to them. Accompanying the gift of sentience is the capacity to choose. Human beings have the ability to choose to be reflections of their ultimate Source.[51] In their own measure, they can establish deep, loving relationships in which to utilize their own creative potentials for the good of others. Following their divine template, they can be selfless and other-oriented. They can freely choose to transcend themselves. This gift of choice also means that they can choose to be self-centered, egocentric, grasping and petty. Such decisions are contrary to the relational life of the Maker and diminish the divine spark that enables life in the One's image.[52]

Perhaps this freedom of will is related to the random aspects of the universe. God has designed temporal creation itself to be free, to be variable. Sentient humans share this unpredictable quality. Perhaps human freedom is related to mortality. The uncertainties about what may lie beyond certain death pose a defining challenge to self-aware mortal minds. They color the exercise of human free will. Each person consciously or unconsciously must choose how to cope with the reality of inevitable death.

### 3. Mortality and Freedom

Over human history, in diverse times and places, there have been various responses to this recognition of the inevitability of personal death. Either consciously or unconsciously, some have tried to ignore this reality. Some felt that their individual deaths were not important compared to the continuation of their kinfolk or their communities. They would be immortal through their people and through their children. Their lives were thus oriented to the well-being of their families and communities.

Others conceived there would be another life in a spiritual realm. They imagined various conditions, sometimes ethical, sometimes through submission and worship, that would have to be fulfilled to enter this afterlife.

Other people lived in cultures that reasoned in a cyclic fashion rather than linearly. They concluded that people passed through cycles of lives in which they were continually reincarnated until achieving ultimate unity with all existence. Progress through these cycles depended on the moral quality of each life.

Still other people sought to deny their mortality by making themselves into immortal gods. Demanding the worship of other people, they hoarded material possessions and established their power through military might. Some required the enslavement or sacrifice of human beings to consolidate their dominance.

Other people concluded that death was the definitive end of their personal existences. The wiser among them reasoned that they should spend their short existences making life better for others, but others fell into the despair that life was utterly meaningless and might as well be lived self-servingly.

And so, for diverse reasons, human freedom of choice was often exercised in an egotistical pursuit of personal gain and power. Whether expressed as an individual's struggle for dominance and wealth or as a tribe's quest for superiority and control of its neighbors, human society became riddled with inducements to selfishness. As new generations were born, they often matured in morally corrosive environments in which the weak were seen to exist as playthings for the strong, and which exalted the use of force and might to achieve desired goals. Human societies were permeated with enticements to sinful decisions. Such choices oppose God's desires for humanity. People became inured to using their capacities in sinful and, ultimately, self-destructive ways.[53]

All these things, though, happened in a world permeated by the mysterious presence of the transcendent One who created and sustained it.[54] Through diverse subtle manifestations, God delicately called and empowered people to choose freely to live in the divine image and so advance God's intentions for the world. God's continuous invitation to relationship was and is mediated in numerous ways. A divine empowerment to perceive and accept this invitation was and is always made available, too. Because of the divine respect for human freedom, revelations of God's calls to relationship are always mutual—they require human decisions to engage with the divine self-disclosure that God initiates. God encourages and empowers this human choice.[55]

Recorded human history and complex organized societies were made possible with the invention of agriculture in various regions of the earth around ten or twelve thousand years ago. The production of surplus amounts of food permitted the rise of cities and city-states. This, in turn, prompted their rulers to develop writing. They also caused the growth of societies in which the lives of most people were controlled by the powerful few. The authority of the rulers was legitimated through the establishment of state religions. The leaders were portrayed as agents of the gods or as deities themselves, entitled to the worship and service of the people they subjugated.

## 4. The Birth of Israel

This story now reaches a major turning point. The relational God had always desired sentient humans to enter freely into relationship with their Creator and so participate in the ongoing unfolding of creation. God had gifted them with the capacity to choose to do so. Never overwhelming this freedom by coercive displays of divine might and majesty, the One had instead subtly summoned people, through countless mediations in the created world, to live in the divine image in which they were fashioned. Now God becomes involved in human history in a special way by forming a distinctive relationship with a particular Semitic people of the Near East. God becomes actively present in time in their flesh.[56]

Over time, the Hebrew people became aware of the One. Inspired and willing to respond to God's divine outreach, they learned to call God by a special name—YHWH—a name of timelessness, of holiness, of otherness, the One who is and who will be. They perceived that this God is not like the alleged deities they had been forced to serve. This is One who desires human beings to live together in societies of justice and peace. This is One concerned about the plight of the weak.

The agrarian Hebrew tribes acquired a vision of what God intends as the ideal human society. Living on the frontier between mighty empires, the Hebrews developed an aversion to powerful rulers who oppress and dominate their subjects. The One alone is king. The land was not to be consolidated under the ownership of a powerful few, but fairly distributed among all the people. Each extended Hebrew family was to be God's steward of an ancestral tract of land, large and arable enough to make the family self-sufficient. Legal customs arose to ensure that loss of land or servitude through indebtedness was never permanent, and laws were enacted to give the poor and weak access to food and shelter.[57] The family had a duty to God to see that they lived according to these ethical standards of justice and honesty. Ritual practices reinforced and intensified these ethical norms. The Hebrews were to worship and thank the One for the blessings of the land and teachings, which defined their distinctive identity.

They were to treat one another, the strangers in their midst, and even their domesticated beasts, with kindness and righteousness. If not, their tenure as tenants on God's land would be imperiled. All these teachings, both oral and written, were understood as expressions of the divine will for intense relationships of justice and mutuality. The Maker's transcendent values and purposes were slowly becoming manifest in the tales and texts of this people particularly open to the God's animating presence.[58] They were learning a way of walking through life that could set them apart from sinful habits and unjust societies.

As time passed, the Hebrews understood that they had entered into a covenant with the One. This idea was initially based on the legal agreements that people made with one another in that time and society. With the passing of the centuries, though, the Hebrew concept of covenant acquired more profound meanings. The name "Israel"—to grapple or wrestle with God—became the name for the Hebrew peoples as a collective unity. It expressed that this people could not be thought of without reference to God, and God could not be fathomed without reference to the People Israel. God is the God of Israel and Israel is the Israel of God.[59] Their existences are entwined. People were being called to live truly in God's image and so participate in the divine intentions for creation.

The Hebrews told stories of how their relationship with God came about. Drawing upon older oral traditions, spoken and written sagas explored how the ancient ancestors of Israel became connected to God in a complex tapestry of divine promises and human responsibility. A pivotal narrative related the escape of the Hebrews from the dominance of a great empire ruled by a deified Pharaoh. God's firstborn children Israel were seen as saved through divine intervention on their behalf and brought to a holy mountain where they entered into a formal covenant and agreed to share life with God. These sagas achieved written form in a complicated pattern of composition and editing, and became the foundation for the reflection and self-definition of Israel forevermore.

## 5. Kings

How much of this developing vision of an ideal Hebrew society was actually achieved is not known. Their precarious location at the crossroads of empires made enduring peace and stability a rare occurrence for them. It was not long before the threat of the invading Philistine people required the compromise of one aspect of their vision. To survive militarily, the Hebrews needed a human commander to oversee the defense of their disparate tribes. So Israel acquired a human king.

This was not an easy development. The Hebrew suspicion of centralizing too much power in a human being conflicted with the urgent need for the rapid and coordinated employment of the Hebrew tribal militias. Written works handed down from this period reveal that an uneasy compromise was attempted. The true sovereign of Israel was God. The human king of Israel was merely God's agent. The king's dependence on God was seen in the fact that he was installed by an anointing ceremony. The king was God's anointed one, God's messiah or instrument, only so long as he ruled according to the ethical standards of the Hebrew tradition. He was not to be another Pharaoh and oppress his own people. He was to respect the ancient tribal leaders and customs. He was to preserve clan and familial possession of the land, and not seek to consolidate property unto himself. Only as long as these limits on his power were observed would a human king be a legitimate ruler over the Israel of God.

The careers of the kings showed the wisdom of the Hebrew fears of a monarchy. Although David acquired a Canaanite city, renamed it Jerusalem and made it his capital, he was conscious of the need to respect Hebrew tribal traditions. Even so, his dynasty was beset by battles within his own family for dominance. His successor Solomon was remembered as being very wise and building the first temple in Jerusalem, but he replaced tribal leaders with his own appointed district governors and levied taxes and impressed labor on his own people. After Solomon's death, most of the Hebrew tribes refused to be ruled any longer by a descendant of David. They established their own rival monarchy in the north. The experiment of a king ruling justly over the twelve tribes of Israel had disintegrated after a dynasty of only two generations. The separate northern and southern Hebrew realms, each ruled by their own king, continued the attempt to develop a just monarchical rule, but with little success. In both nations, the kings sought to seize control of tribal lands. They supported the worship of the gods of other countries in an effort to build a network of military alliances. As with their kings, many of the people also departed from Hebrew ideals. Thus, the distinctiveness of the Hebrew vision and society became blurred. Eventually, the monarchies would be destroyed by attacks from foreign superpowers: Assyria in the case of northern Israel and Babylon in the case of southern Judah.

## 6. Prophets

Prophets arose in response to monarchical abuses. Over the centuries, in different ways and with different tactics, these men and women confronted the sins they saw in Israelite and Judean society. They were the guardians and developers of the Hebrew vision, the consciences of the covenant, summoning the kings and leaders in particular to live according to the ethical norms of the God of Israel.[60] Elijah, Amos, Hosea, Isaiah, and Jeremiah are among the prophets whose careers were commemorated and interpreted in written texts that have been handed down to the present. Further insights into life with God were thereby preserved for the future.

In the face of repeated violations of covenantal principles, some of the prophets began to long for a day when things would be set right. Some of them expected that one day God would call forth a king who would finally rule, according to God's will, with justice and integrity.[61] Some imagined a time when the whole world would be at peace and even the animals would no longer kill one another. They perceived that everything that existed would ultimately conform to the Maker's intentions. As time passed, the Jewish people came to believe that the present age would give way to an Age to Come in which the God of love, justice, and relationship would reign over a cosmos where peace, justice, wholeness, and mutually empowering relationships would prevail. God intended Israel to assist in bringing this all about.

## 7. Priests

The conquest of Judah by Babylon and the subsequent exile of its leaders proved to be the catalyst for tremendous spiritual creativity among the people of Israel. In coming to grips with this national disaster, exiled prophets reflected upon Israel's life in an international context. Confidence that God would not let Israel's story be over seems to have appeared after the initial trauma had subsided. As part of its covenant with the One, Israel had a divine mission to fulfill. Israel was meant by God to be a light to the nations of the world. By witnessing the divine sharing of life with Israel, the Gentile nations would come to recognize the sovereignty of the One. They would become eager to enter into relationship with God, too.

After the Persian Empire conquered the Babylonians, the exiles were free to go back to Judea. Some remained in Babylon as part of a Judean community that would prosper there for centuries. Those who returned to Jerusalem began the rebuilding of their nation. Since their Persian overlords would not permit the continued existence of a monarchy, the temple priestly aristocracy governed the society that developed. The priests, in their various classes, had a way of viewing the world that emphasized the holiness of God. This was reflected in the sacred rituals they practiced. Those desiring to enter the divine presence abiding in the temple would need to be properly prepared, properly purified for their encounter with the Holy One. Blood, seen as the tangible vessel of the divine animating spark, was understood to reinvigorate or restore the living covenantal bond between the Israel of God and the God of Israel. Consequently, the priestly rituals centered on animal sacrifices of thanksgiving, petition, or penitence to God in which sacred blood was carefully used to reinvigorate covenantal relationship.

The postexilic priestly classes engaged in tremendous literary activity. Partially concerned to codify the ritual operations of the temple, they were probably also motivated by the disaster of the exile to preserve Israel's oral and written traditions. They collected, combined, and edited numerous written texts. They composed major new works of their own. In these years, many of the books of the later Jewish Tanakh and the Christian Bible achieved their final forms, most notably the five books of the Torah—Genesis, Exodus, Leviticus, Numbers, and Deuteronomy—as well as collections of prophetic works and of Israel's hymns and poems in the Psalter.[62]

Thus, under priestly rule earlier Israelite traditions were preserved and revised. Israel understood itself to be called by God to holiness, to an ethical and ritual life that would set it apart from other peoples. Dietary regulations and the observance of the weekly Sabbath were among the practices that fostered Jewish identity and relationship to God.

Some priests understood this call to a distinctive life in an insular, exclusivist way—God's people should avoid being contaminated by others. Others cautioned that God was concerned about all people and that goodness and righteousness were to be found among the Gentiles as well. They wrote stories such as those of Ruth and Jonah to make these points, recalling the prophetic tradition that Israel was to be a light to the nations.

The nature of Israel's covenantal life with God had become clearer. God would not permit Israel to disappear, but would remain faithful to Israel even in the face of deserved or undeserved calamity. God was perpetually committed to advancing divine purposes in the world through this chosen people. The One would always bring new life and growth to the remnants of the people of Israel, guiding them ever in their role in the divine relationship. They had a task to help bring creation to its ultimate destiny.

## 8. Greece and Rome

The relatively benign rule of the Persians ended when Alexander the Great of Macedonia conquered the land of Israel, bringing with him the robust Greek civilization. The Greeks considered their culture to be superior to those of the other peoples they encountered. They felt that they were bringing the gift of a refined and mature civilization to the barbarians whom they dominated. They saw themselves establishing a worldwide and cosmopolitan culture that all people should welcome.

The arrival of Greek perspectives and values caused much division among the ruling classes of Jerusalem. Some priests welcomed Greek philosophy and learning, and sought to assimilate them into the new international society. They constructed Greek gymnasiums and theatres, wore Greek clothing, and adopted Greek names. Others studied Greek literature and were attracted by it, but they deemed their ancient Hebrew traditions to be superior. Some would seek to explain and articulate Israelite ideas using the concepts and thought categories of Greek philosophy and metaphysics. They concluded that Israel's holy texts expressed the wisdom of the divine One and were therefore superior even to the refined notions of the Greeks. Still other priests and their scribal assistants, faced with the attractive power of Greek sophistication, feared a loss of Judean identity. Recalling how the corrupt Hebrew kings had consorted with pagan gods and so were destroyed, they condemned assimilationists for abandoning the traditions of their ancestors.

By this time, the descendants of ancient Israel lived in widely scattered places, dispersed in what came to be called the diaspora. Jewish communities could be found from Babylon to northern Africa to Greece and further into northern and western Europe. For many of them, Greek became their primary language. Consequently, scholars in the city of Alexandria, Egypt, translated the sacred texts of ancient Israel into Greek.

The conflicts among the various responses to Greek culture came to a head when a certain Hellenistic king used force to stamp out Judean practices and to put the image of a pagan god in the temple. Armed insurrection broke out among the Israelite traditionalists, led by a family called the Hasmoneans. Because of the international political situation, they succeeded in throwing off Greek rule. A century-long independent Judean rule under the Hasmoneans began.

Great divisions in Judean society marked the Hasmonean period. The Hasmonean family made itself kings, chief priests, and military commanders. The former priestly leadership condemned this usurpation of their authority. Some of them abandoned the Jerusalem they deemed to be hopelessly corrupt and established a singular covenantal community, a true Israel, in the wilderness near the Dead Sea. Others turned to the sacred texts of Israel and began to read them in new ways in the light of the encounter with Greek culture. Among them were the Pharisees who would come to interpret the Torah creatively in order to make daily life as holy as the activities in the temple. Within the Hasmonean family itself there was conflict as rival claimants to the throne contended with one another and sought alliances with foreign powers to bolster their positions. Although Judean rule expanded to include regions not controlled since Solomon's day, the land was troubled by the battles raging among the dynastic competitors. Eventually, one foreign ally stepped in and assumed control of the region. Thus the land came under the growing power of Rome.

Working through indigenous client-kings, the Romans proved to be efficient overlords. To govern in Judea and northern Galilee, the Romans appointed a clever chieftain from the land to the south of Judea, who was afterwards called Herod the Great. For thirty-three years Herod reigned as King of the Jews, styling himself as both the fulfillment of Judean hopes for a king like David of old and as the ideal Greco-Roman client-king. As such he engaged in extensive and expensive building projects. Recalling Solomon, he magnificently enlarged and renovated the temple, but according to Roman architectural forms. He founded or restored numerous cities and fortresses, including the deep-water seaport of Caesarea Maritima, equipped with Roman theatres and temples. He also dedicated monuments to Caesar elsewhere in the empire. His subjects had to provide revenues for the maintenance of the temple, the costs of Herod's various building projects, and the biannual tribute of 25 percent of their produce to Rome itself.

Upon Herod's death, the empire divided his realm among his sons. One of them was quickly replaced by a Roman official as governor over Judea and Samaria, but Herod Antipas, as ruler over Galilee to the north and Perea, east of the Jordan River, continued his father's fondness for building projects. He rebuilt the city of Sepphoris as his first capital in Galilee, but later constructed an entirely new capital of Tiberias on the shores of the Lake of Galilee. Galileans, the descendants of the northern Hebrew tribes, thus came into intense, direct contact with Greco-Roman culture in their own territory.

At this time, there were many varieties of religious practices and a number of renewal movements among the people of Israel. The Sadducees who, under Roman oversight helped direct the operations of the Jerusalem temple, debated with less literally-minded Pharisees about the proper interpretation of the Torah. The Pharisees, in turn, had their own internal disputes about correct purity and dietary observances. The priestly community by the Dead Sea dismissed other groups as corrupt or untrustworthy. The vast number of Judean and Galilean peasants had issues of indebtedness and loss of land to face. Popular prophetic figures and charismatic preachers enjoined their fellow peasants that God would soon bring justice to Israel.

It was in this dynamic and contentious time that there arose in the little Galilean village of Nazareth another charismatic preacher and healer named Jesus. His mission on behalf of the God of Israel would lead to the birth of the church, bursting out from Israel and taking root throughout the Gentile empire of the Romans.

## 9. Jesus the Galilean

Jesus was raised in the popular traditions of Israel in a little village only a few miles from Antipas's first capital of Sepphoris. He probably grew up learning tales of northern tribal heroes such as Elijah and Elisha. Because he lived close to the land, the ancient Hebrew ideals of familial self-sufficiency as tenants upon the land owned by God were palpable realities for him. He shared in the hopes and dreams of his fellow villagers as they looked upon Galilee and saw the increasingly pervasive presence of Roman rule.[63]

As an adult, Jesus became acquainted with a popular prophet named John. Preaching at the Jordan River like Joshua of old, John called the people of Israel back to their roots in the wilderness. He declared that God would soon be coming in judgment to bring justice into the world. God's people needed to make themselves ready for this. Recalling the tales of Israel's entry into the land, he invited his listeners to immerse themselves in the Jordan in a purifying baptism and so pass through its waters with a renewed commitment to living according to Israel's covenantal principles. Jesus, too, participated in this baptism. He was convinced that God was active on Israel's behalf.

John was executed by Antipas as a disturber of the Roman peace. Shortly afterward, Jesus began his own public activity, announcing that the Kingdom of God was dawning. His ministry powerfully combined both past and future and so transformed the present. Embodying Israel's covenantal life with God, Jesus confronted his time like the heroic prophets of the past. He summoned the people to a renewed commitment of sharing life with God as described in the Torah and the traditions of Israel. Through welcoming fellowship meals, through healings and restorations, and through symbolic deeds that announced Israel's renewal, he offered a foretaste of life in the Age to Come. As a supremely faithful son of Israel, he walked in God's way so potently that the Reign of God was made effectively present and the end of the present evil age could be tangibly felt.

But Israel's long covenant had shown that human societies habituated to sin would rise up against the fulfillment of God's designs. As the Jewish people had experienced calamity and disaster and exile at the hands of the Gentile nations, so Jesus in his own life repeated that pattern. The Roman overlords and their puppets among the temple priesthood captured Jesus when he was not among the people. The Romans tortured him to death as a pretender "King of the Jews." His closest companions fled and despaired. It appeared that his story had ended. But just as Jesus embodied the persecuted experiences of Israel, he was also revealed as incarnating Israel's covenanting experiences of restoration.

## 10. A Confirming Revelation

Jesus' companions were shattered by his death. The tangible presence of the Age to Come that he demonstrated had been overwhelmed by the very evils that were supposed to vanish in the New Creation. Then the disciples of Jesus began to undergo a revelation. They started to experience their crucified friend as still alive, not in an ordinary, everyday fashion, but transcendently. Particularly when they gathered for their customary fellowship meals, now memorials to Jesus' faithfulness to God even to the point of death, they came to feel his abiding presence among them.[64] As a revelation, as a divine invitation to relationship directed specifically at them, these encounters generated a human affirmation empowered by God. The experiences of the Crucified One continuing to live in transcendent glory both required and produced a faith response in his friends. The conviction that the crucified Jesus had been raised to transcendent glory was an unexpected and stunning instance of a divine restoration of Israel after calamity. The supremely faithful God of Israel who never forgets the covenanting partner had resurrected the supremely faithful Son of Israel. This staggering development caused the disciples of Jesus to struggle to understand the meaning of what had occurred. They consulted the texts and traditions of Israel and sought to grasp and express this new thing that the One had done.[65]

They saw that Jesus' deeds, death, and resurrection had reaffirmed and begun to achieve the Kingdom of God that Jesus had proclaimed. They continued to experience in Jesus the life of the

Age to Come in which he now existed.[66] They understood that death itself would be overcome in God's Reign.

They gathered together for celebrations of this experience and formed assemblies, or churches, of believers in Jesus as crucified and raised. In their initial enthusiasm the first generation of these believers felt that the Age to Come must be about to arrive in all its fullness. As time passed, though, they came to the realization that God had other plans and that they had an ongoing mission to perform in the world. Empowered by his living presence, they were to continue Jesus' ministry of preparing the world for the Kingdom of God.

Those who experienced the Exalted Crucified One also reflected deeply on the identity of Jesus himself. As one who fully embodied Israel's covenanting life with God, he was indeed "the King of the Jews," as mockingly declared by the Romans. His resurrection demonstrated that he was certainly an anointed agent or messiah of God, as any king of Israel would be. But their experience of the Crucified and Raised One eclipsed any of the diverse messianic expectations that circulated among Jews of the time. The word *messiah* did not adequately convey their overwhelming encounter with the Exalted One. Particularly in its Greek form, *Christ,* Jesus as messiah quickly dwindled in importance as a descriptive title, becoming instead part of his name. "Jesus Christ" thus expressed the totality of encountering Jesus during his Galilean ministry as well as in his martyrdom and vindication by being exalted to transcendence. *Christ* expressed the disciples' experience of God's invitation to relationship personified in Jesus. When the church today confesses Jesus as Christ, it testifies to the ongoing, covenantal sharing-in-life with God that was established, is sustained, and continues to be experienced through Jesus' life, death, and glorious transformation.

Those who experienced Jesus as crucified and raised also expected that he would soon return in glory and majesty to usher in the Kingdom of God in whose service he had given his entire life. They adapted previous Pharisaic ideas about a general resurrection of the dead at the dawning of the Age to Come to articulate the novelty of their experiences. They understood the transcendent resurrection of Jesus to be proof that the Reign of God was indeed beginning. They anticipated that he would participate in God's power to judge the living and the dead as the Age to Come was definitively established. In their gatherings, they began singing about Jesus Christ as the enthroned "Lord" who would transform the world and institute divine justice. In retrospect, they realized that God had been encountered in Jesus' life and death and that God was communing with them through the Raised One. Drawing upon the wealth of images in the traditions of Israel, they conceived of Jesus' life and death in terms of the ultimate prophet who died for his message, as the Wisdom of God rejected by ignorant humanity, as the Suffering Servant whose pains brought unexpected blessing, and, using the priestly language of the temple, as the superlative sacrifice that atoned for sin. They expressed their discovery of Jesus' significance and identity in various ways, addressing him as God's Wisdom, God's Word, God's Lamb, and God's Son. In praising Jesus in these words today, the church proclaims that God's characteristic outreach for relationship has been and continues to be most powerfully experienced through him. It also proclaims that he will inevitably bring into being God's Peaceable Kingdom for the entire world.

## 11. A Distinctive Community

The proclamation of the death and exaltation of Jesus Christ, the Son of the Living God, began to be spread by Jewish apostles or emissaries of the good news as evidence of the New Age that was breaking into human history. The apostles traveled out into the diaspora, telling their fellow Jews about what God was accomplishing in and through Jesus Christ. New churches of believers in the lordship of Jesus began to form. Adapting Jewish purification rituals and recalling the practice of John in the Jordan, a ritual immersion, or baptism, was the initiation of newcomers into this assembly of the Coming Age. Members of the church celebrated their participation in God's nascent Kingdom by continuing the table fellowship that they had shared with Jesus during his ministry. Now, however, that meal memorialized and gave thanks for his life, death, exaltation, and triumphant return. During the meal, the presence of the Exalted One could be felt. It came to be called the Lord's Supper or the Eucharist, meaning thanksgiving.

The earliest apostles were not fully prepared to respond when it was non-Jewish Gentiles who most warmly received their message. Some of these Gentiles had already become acquainted with the God of Israel because of the witness of Israel in the diaspora. They had adopted some Jewish customs and informally participated in Jewish religious observances. These "God-fearers" included some who were very curious about the good news preached by the apostles. They wanted to participate in the local church assemblies that were coalescing.

The apostles were confronted with a crisis. Should Gentiles be admitted to their gatherings, and, if so, under what conditions and expectations? Before his death, Jesus had never discussed such a question. A range of views is evident in the writings of the earliest churches. Those who advocated a welcoming stance toward the Gentiles recalled the inclusiveness of Jesus' fellowship meals at which all were gladly received, despite their reputations or lack of ritual purity. They also pointed out that the Gentiles' interest must be the result of divine empowerment and invitation. It was an action by God that the apostles could not oppose. Local churches began to admit Gentiles into their fellowship, although there were diverse requirements for admission for many years.

The experience of inclusion in church assemblies seems to have been a powerful one for these newly received Gentiles. They sensed that their relationship with God in Christ was of an equal status with those Jews who had preceded them. They felt themselves truly to be people of God, set apart from a sinful world. The divisions of class, education, gender, and social status that fragmented people in Roman society were experienced as irrelevant in an assembly in which all were one. They felt empowered to devote themselves to the standards of Israel, mediated to them through the Jewish members of the church. Although there were disputes and controversies and failures to live up to the church's ideals, Gentiles in significant numbers sought admission. Through the apostleship of wandering missionaries such as Paul of Tarsus, largely Gentile churches began to form throughout the eastern Roman Empire.

To the Jewish apostles of Jesus Christ, this Gentile enthusiasm was yet another confirmation that the Kingdom of God was dawning and that the climax of the covenant was at hand. Israel's mission to be a light to the Gentile nations was being accomplished through the apostolic preaching of Jesus crucified and raised. Relationship with the God of Israel and knowledge of Israel's ethical way of life were being spread and adopted throughout the known world. Letters written to and from the nascent churches and gospels that narrated the story of Jesus crucified and exalted were composed. They were later collected into a canon of scriptures that would be the basis of Christian self-understanding forevermore.

Some Jews who did not experience the revelation of God in Christ began to wonder about the new Jesus movement and the growth of the Jewish-Gentile churches. Was a novel type of contact with the Gentile world eroding Jewish identity and distinctiveness? Perhaps instead of introducing Gentiles to the ways of Israel, Jews were being assimilated into Gentile culture. It is likely that some Jews in the churches also began to have such thoughts as the number of new Jewish members declined and the influx of Gentiles grew.

Some Jews who were not members of local church assemblies began to have other concerns. Not having shared in the revelation of the Crucified One as exalted, and not experiencing covenantal life with God mediated through Jesus' transcendent presence, these Jews became alarmed by references to Jesus as the Lord and Son of God. Was a human individual being divinized? Was Israel's foundational conviction that there was one God and one God alone being compromised by the church's prayers and songs to the Raised One? Did the church believe that there were two divinities, not one? The novelty of the church's experience of Christ and the growing presence of Gentiles in the churches were beginning to lead to the birth of a separate religion.

The Gentiles brought with them into the church their own ways of looking at life. Some would especially relate to Jesus' death in terms of the Greco-Roman cultural themes of a hero's self-chosen and transformative death or in terms of a vicarious and sacrificial dying to appease the gods. Some powerfully experienced having been brought from darkness to light, from sin to sanctity, from isolation to peoplehood. They developed distinctive understandings of having been saved. Some Gentiles saw no need to observe the ritual practices of Israel, while others continued to do so for many centuries. Other Gentiles were inclined to think according to the metaphysical categories of Greek philosophies and began to ponder the relationship between God and Jesus Christ in terms of their divine *ontos,* or being.

These developments were impacted by the outbreak of Jewish revolts against the Roman Empire. All of the diverse kinds of Jews, and their Gentile admirers, were shocked by the catastrophic conclusion to the first revolt. The great temple in Jerusalem was destroyed and reduced to rubble. The ancient center of Hebrew and Jewish ritual life was gone. There could, at least for the present, be no more pilgrimages to Mount Zion for the great festivals of Passover, Pentecost, and Tabernacles. No more opportunities for a holy, spiritual journey to Mount Zion. There would be no more joyous singing of the Psalms of Ascent when Jews from around the world entered into the glorious house of God. Hopes that the temple might be swiftly rebuilt were squashed when another revolt was defeated. Jews were forbidden from entering the once-holy city that was now dedicated to Roman deities. But, as had happened before in Israel's covenantal life, occasions of disaster set the stage for renewal and rebirth. Two covenantal movements would emerge from the ashes of the wars: Christianity and Rabbinic Judaism.

After the destruction of the temple, the ritual and liturgical practices of the priests could no longer be observed. A defining feature of Israel's covenanting life had disappeared. There already existed other Jewish ways of celebrating the One's presence, forgiveness, and love. These would now need to be enhanced and further refined.

Priestly scribes who copied and preserved Israel's sacred scriptures could use them as the basis for anchoring Israel's identity until such time as the temple might be rebuilt. Various groups of Pharisees had earlier begun to extend temple holiness out into the wider world beyond its walls. Their initiative was intensified now that the temple was no more. Jews living in the diaspora also had the experience of not having the temple as the focus of their religious life. The ancient scriptures, long ago translated into Greek, had already begun to serve as the basis of a text-based, rather than sacrifice-based, spirituality. Jews who participated in the churches saw yet another way to reshape Jewish spirituality and life. They claimed that the covenant fully expressed in Jesus' life, death, and exaltation was the way that God now wanted the people of Israel to live. These and other approaches to cope with the loss of the temple vied with one another for advantage and dominance for many years.

The church's gospels were written during this period. These narratives told the story of Jesus' ministry from the perspectives of various local church communities who experienced Christ's living presence among them.[67] The different opinions on Gentile admission and the competition for preeminence with diversified Jewish groups after the fall of the temple are evident in their pages. In telling of Jesus' execution by the Romans, the gospel writers tended to downplay the responsibility of the Roman prefect and to enlarge upon the role played the Jewish people and their leaders. This was partially the result of the debates between Jews inside and outside the church, but also because of the need to present the church in the best possible light to the Romans, under whose rule it had to live.[68] Thus for many reasons, members of the church, now increasingly called "Christians," were becoming more and more distinct and separated from the diverse Jewish communities.

Several factors contributed in different ways at different places to this separation. The church's claims about Jesus, the growing presence of Gentiles, the refusal of Christians to hail the leader of the second Judean revolt as messiah, and an economic incentive for Christians to define themselves as non-Jewish to avoid paying a special tax levied against Jews—all these encouraged the formation of boundaries between Jews and Christians.

## 12. Rabbinic Judaism

Over the centuries after the loss of Jerusalem, two centers of Jewish learning became enormously important. In Galilee and in Babylon scribes now called "rabbis" began to put into writing traditions that had been circulating among some of them for years. Studying and reflecting in a world without a temple, they related these traditions to the scriptures of ancient Israel in creative and powerful ways. Works such as the Mishnah and two Talmuds established the basis for an ongoing conversation across the centuries about how to live in covenant with God. Although it took many years for this to occur, eventually the rabbis' way of being Jewish would become normative for all the scattered descendants of ancient Israel.

The rabbis emphasized the duty of each Jew to walk according to the commands, or *mitzvoth,* of God as expressed in the Torah and interpreted through the rabbinic traditions. The Torah took on a cosmic significance for the rabbis; it was the divine plan with which the world was created. Nature was a manifestation of Torah. By living a Torah-life, one would be in harmony with existence itself. The study and discussion of the Torah and the commentaries upon it thus became a defining activity in rabbinic

Judaism. A mystical strand of rabbinic reflection also flourished. Subsequent centuries of innovative rabbinic thought testified to the ongoing creativity and dynamism of Judaism.

The rabbis understood God's creation to be incomplete. They looked toward the Age to Come envisioned by the ancient Hebrew prophets as the culmination to which all existence was moving. Medieval rabbis felt that those who lived in covenant with God had a mission to mend the world, to help bring the world to the completion intended by the One. This could be done through the observance of the *mitzvoth* of charity, justice, ritual, and prayer, but these precepts had to be performed out of love and gratitude to the One who had deigned to share covenanting life with Israel.

The observance of the Sabbath rest was perceived as an anticipation of the peace and righteousness that would characterize the Age to Come. This weekly refreshing in God's presence served to reorient God's people to their identity and mission in the world. Jewish seasonal festivals of thanksgiving, recommitment, penitence, and renewal, now even more centered in the home and local community, celebrated the people's ongoing covenantal bonding with God.

The loss of the temple meant that the intense, holy presence of God was not to be found in a specific place or building. Later rabbis realized that the absence of God in a holy shrine meant that God was paradoxically even more pervasively present throughout the world, though elusively and indirectly. They concluded that God was now relying more heavily on the human covenantal partners to be lights to the nations by sanctifying the world and hallowing life through the loving enactment of the *mitzvoth.*[69]

The achievement of the earliest rabbis was remarkable. Some have suggested that it enabled the people of Israel to thrive in widely divergent places and periods and contributed to their survival in the face of later persecutions. Their work informs Jewish life down to the present day.

## 13. Christianity in the Roman World

The separating Jewish and Christian communities initially faced very different situations in the Roman Empire. After the catastrophe of their revolts, Jews settled into a fairly prosperous life in the diaspora. They were officially recognized as a legal religious group and were exempt from worshipping Roman deities. Some Jewish communities undertook extensive synagogue building projects. They were vital parts of the social life of their towns and cities. Some Gentiles, including Christians, found Jewish ways very attractive. Jewish ethical standards, communal solidarity, ancient religious practices, and dignified rituals were all very appealing. Christians, in contrast, had a low social status. Subject to popular disdain and periodic persecutions, the church craved acceptance in an empire in which some charged that it was only a heretical deviation from Judaism.

To respond to such charges and to combat Judaism's attractiveness for its own members, church leaders denigrated Judaism. They began to devise an anti-Jewish theology that would influence Christian thinking for over a millennium. Taking argumentative passages from the gospels and other Christian texts,[70] and reading the internal criticisms of the Hebrew prophets as evidence of constant Jewish failures, Christian teachers began to instruct that Jews were no longer in covenant with God.[71] That status had been transferred to the church. Therefore the Jews had lost their homeland and their temple. Although they should not be attacked or killed, the Jews were now doomed to homeless wandering because of their slaying of the messiah whom God had sent. The Jewish Torah, referred to as the Law, had likewise been replaced by the law of love brought by Christ. The relationship of the two fledgling communities of Christianity and Rabbinic Judaism came to be premised upon the belief that for one tradition to be legitimate, the other had to be in error.

At this same time, the church found that it had to respond to emerging doctrinal questions and to articulate its beliefs according to the prevailing philosophical categories of Greek metaphysics. The Hebrew tradition, and the Christian and Jewish religious communities descended from it, tended to conceive of reality in terms of how it was experienced in people's lives and in human history. God became known through the experiences of dwelling in divine covenantal relationship. Greek ontological philosophy, on the other hand, tended to be concerned with a logical system of thought that explained how everything interconnected on the level of their very being. It also was inclined to think in terms of dichotomous categories. The Transcendent was by definition unknowable to mortals except through the agency of a mediating Word, or *Logos,* that bridged the gap between the mortal and divine realms.

Challenged by questioners who thought in such terms, Christian leaders had to develop ways of conceiving the truths of their faith using ontological categories. Jesus Christ was described as the divine *Logos* that mediates the divine to humanity. God was described according to the abstract characteristics of omniscience, omnipresence, and omnipotence, and not always in the relational way of the Hebrew tradition.

This theological move into Greek metaphysics was not without its problems. Equating Jesus Christ with the *Logos* threatened at times to overwhelm the real humanity of Jesus the Galilean. There were disputes for centuries over how to use Greek dichotomous categories to assert both the humanity and the divinity of Jesus Christ. How Christ as the Son related to the Father and to the Holy Spirit without violating monotheism was a very difficult question. Different centers of Christian learning in Antioch, Alexandria, Constantinople, and Rome debated doctrinal formulations. Nonetheless, even while these disputations were seething both within and without the church, the numbers of Christians steadily increased. The church's organizational structure was coalescing. Rich liturgical practices and creative sermons based upon them provided powerful experiences of God to members of the Christian community.

However, the stability of the Roman Empire began to decline during this period. Ancient tensions between the Latin-speaking western empire and the Greek-speaking eastern empire were becoming more evident. The Roman infrastructure was deteriorating. New populations began pressuring the empire from the outside.

Eventually, the Emperor Constantine saw the growing church as one means by which the unity of the empire might be strengthened. He himself became a Christian. The church was no longer at terrible risk in the empire. Constantine was so concerned about the unity within the church and the empire that he convened a council at Nicea to settle one of the divisive christological debates that had been raging for years.

Although not every imperial successor to Constantine was a Christian, within a few decades Christianity would become the preferred state religion of the Roman Empire. Huge numbers of people sought baptism as a means of entering the imperial governmental establishment. This demand brought enormous changes in Christian worship and practice. Large edifices needed to be constructed to accommodate the burgeoning numbers of Christian worshippers. Christian bishops became part of the Roman legal system and dressed accordingly. In a few centuries the church had gone from a persecuted sect held in general disrepute to become the heart of a mighty Christian empire. To some it seemed that the Kingdom of God on earth had been realized at last.

Imperial power brought with it new possibilities, but also new perils. Just as Israel of old met with both success and failure in attempting to establish a just society under God's rule, so too the church would both succeed and fail in its historical deeds. The prospect of bringing Christ's revelation to the numerous "barbarian" tribes that began to enter the empire fired many Christian missionaries and preachers with great zeal. However, some Christian leaders also used the legal mechanisms of the empire to marginalize competing religious groups, including their old rivals, the Jews. As time passed, Jews were slowly barred from Roman courts and offices and from access to imperial society.

*14. The Middle Ages*

The forces that encouraged the disintegration of the Roman Empire proved to be overwhelming. In the west, the empire collapsed into petty states ruled by tribal strongmen. Battles among migrating masses of people were the norm. Local lords defended their small territories against rivals and newcomers. Centralized authority disappeared, roads and commercial trading were abandoned.

The church was one institution that survived the breakdown of Roman culture. In the east, the structures of empire endured for centuries in the Byzantine Empire, and the eastern church prospered there. In the west, bishops often took on secular authority as local rulers, but ignorance and superstition prevailed in all levels of society, including among the clergy. In the chaos, Christian monasteries were islands of stability, and literacy and learning were preserved in them. Some of these monasteries were established by monks from Ireland, which, being on the fringes of the Roman Empire, had escaped some of the destruction of its collapse. These monasteries served as bases from which preachers launched missions to bring newly arriving Germanic, and later Norse, peoples into the church. Over many centuries, these vast multitudes became slowly integrated into the church's covenant with God. Some of these pagans were eager to adopt the religion of the old empire as part of a process of adopting Roman ways and civilization. They brought with them their own religious customs, some of which entered into the fabric of Christian practice.

Western Christian theology and liturgy were also influenced by the feudalism that gradually emerged in western Europe. Feudal society was organized into various classes that were connected by an interlocking series of debts and protections, from peasant serfs up through local chieftains to the nobility and eventually kings. This structure shaped some of the religious ideas of this period. People saw their relationship to God as a series of debts and graces mediated through the sacraments of the church.

Given the instabilities of the era, there was also an understandable tendency to spiritualize God's Kingdom into a personal afterlife. It was thought that each Christian should seek the grace to overcome their sinful natures and so be rewarded by escaping the vale of tears of this world to be with God forever in the next world.

As landowning nobility, bishops were also part of this hierarchy of governance. This led to certain abuses. In some places local secular rulers appointed bishops on the basis of patronage. In other places, bishops hoarded lands and wealth to pass on to their sons. Largely at the insistence of the Bishops of Rome, the popes, only unmarried men from monasteries were ordained as bishops and celibacy for the lower clergy became the norm. Efforts were also made to standardize the administration of the sacraments and to improve the education of priests. As European society began to reorganize itself, church-sponsored universities eventually emerged.

During the Middle Ages a definitive separation between the eastern and western branches of Christianity occurred. Following the fault-lines that had divided the old Roman Empire, solidarity between the eastern and western churches diminished. Governance, theology, and practice became sufficiently distinctive that topics of dispute frequently erupted into ecclesiastical warfare. Ultimately, in a series of mutual excommunications, East and West parted ways.[72] The Western, or Roman, Church maintained a hierarchical structure with the pope at its apex, while the Eastern, or Orthodox, Churches were organized under the authority of regional patriarchs. From that point on, relations between Eastern and Western Christianity were typically hostile and competitive, occasionally exploding into violence, as when Western crusaders pillaged the Eastern capital of Byzantium.

As Christian society, or Christendom, had become established in the west, the lives of Jews there became increasingly marginalized. As the Middle Ages unfolded, Jews were gradually limited to trading and money-lending pursuits. This filled a valuable and needed economic role in lands recovering from the fall of the empire, but it left Jews dependent on the good will of Christian rulers for their safety. Branded by the old anti-Jewish theological tradition as Christ-killers and homeless wanderers, Jews were periodically expelled from this or that territory as a means of canceling the debts owed to them or in order to remove a perceived threat to Christian purity. When the popes eventually summoned princes to send armies to liberate the ancient land of Israel from the domination of Islamic sovereigns, it was European Jews who were often the first targets of the zealous crusaders. Existing at the margins of medieval society, Jews were scapegoated and accused of ridiculous crimes, including the slaying of Christian children on Passover and poisoning wells in order to cause the Black Plague. Some Christian preachers were instrumental in causing the torture and massacre of local Jewish communities, although other Christian leaders and bishops tried to defend them. These protectors, though, found it difficult to overcome Christendom's caricature of Jews as enemies of God. In various times and places, Jews were threatened with death if they did not accept Christian baptism. Sometimes Jewish children were forcibly taken from their parents to be raised as Christians. Jews who converted to Christianity were often spied upon and then subjected to inquisitorial persecution when suspected of continuing Jewish practices.[73]

Nonetheless, Jewish creativity and learning continually prospered. Scholarly rabbis continued the tradition of commenting upon the Talmudic texts, and Jewish liturgy and culture grew and developed in places where peace prevailed for centuries. Jewish life was especially enriched by its contacts with the Islamic world in the southern Mediterranean, the Iberian peninsula, and Mesopotamia. Islam had begun early in Europe's Middle Ages by Mohammed in Arabia. Partially grounded in Jewish and Christian teachings, Islam is a monotheistic religion dedicated to the worship of the God of Israel. Islam had spread throughout the southern Mediterranean and Middle East by the time of the schism between Eastern and Western Christianity. The Muslims were generally tolerant of the practice of other religious traditions in the lands under their control. Some Islamic and Jewish scholars conducted extensive work on the ancient writings of Aristotle. When their work became known in the Christian West, it sparked a renewal of learning there.

The influence of this rediscovery of Aristotle is most apparent in the works of Thomas Aquinas. He attempted to explain and systematize Christian doctrines and teachings using Aristotelian categories. Although initially deemed questionable by his contemporaries, Aquinas's monumental writings with their systematic, philosophical approach were tremendously influential in the Christian West.

By this time, Europe had begun to emerge from the setbacks of the preceding centuries. In the stability that ensued, a revival of classical civilization occurred. During this Renaissance, or rebirth, trade and exploration expanded, education spread, and the arts flourished. Art and music revolved around Christian themes and images. Princes and bishops, particularly the popes, became patrons of the arts. Masterpieces of painting, sculpture, and music were created. The human form and the natural world were celebrated. As commerce and trade expanded, a wealthy middle class began to appear. The vale of tears was yielding to an age of prosperity.

Throughout all of their history, both Jewish and Christian peoples experienced covenanting life with God amid changing circumstances. Both traditions creatively adapted and responded to the crises and opportunities caused by the end of the Roman Empire in order to continue to live out their faith-relationship in the world. Jews continued to discover God in their engagement with the Torah and rabbinic writings, and they celebrated their relationship with the divine in festivals, holy days, family customs, and literature. Christians continued to experience God through Christ and celebrated their relationship with the divine through developing liturgical and sacramental rites and through art and architecture. Both communities, in different ways, faced specific challenges and temptations in their living out of covenantal life. For example, Jews had to deal with the spiritual and emotional consequences of regular marginalization and periodic victimization in European society. Christians, on the other hand, had to struggle with persistent inclinations toward arrogance, triumphalism, and abuse of power. As was the case with the ancient Hebrews, both groups experienced successes and failures in coping with their particular issues. Despite their flaws, both communities slowly continued to advance God's intentions for the destiny of the world.

## 15. A Reforming Era

The Renaissance in Europe prepared for and anticipated the era of exploration, invention, and immense change that followed. European society was tremendously affected by the rise of the scientific method. This was a procedure for studying reality that required research and the experimental demonstration of hypotheses about the phenomena of nature. Astronomy was one field in which rapid developments occurred. The invention of the telescope and its application to celestial observations resulted in the demise of a long-lived earth-centered view of the universe. A heliocentric model in which the planets, including the earth, were understood to orbit around the sun replaced it. The mathematical formulation of the physical principles governing planetary movements permitted the discovery over the next few centuries of previously unknown planets in the solar system. Europeans using the scientific method became confident that given time they would be able, through empirical investigations, to comprehend and describe all the governing mechanisms of nature.

The initial discoveries that resulted from the use of this method received mixed reactions from certain quarters of the church. Some saw the new discoveries as threatening truths that for centuries had been taken for granted as part of Christian teaching. Occasionally church officials took repressive measures against those utilizing scientific methods.[74]

Several important devices were invented at this time, some of which transformed European society. In particular, the printing press encouraged the rise of literacy and made possible the wide dissemination of new ideas. The first work mass-produced by the printers was the Christian Bible. This publication had an explosive impact in the church. People could compare the biblical accounts of the original churches with their contemporary experience of church. Some found the enthusiasm and fervor of the first Christians lacking in their own church. Some experienced the Bible's narrative presentation of the good news as extremely powerful, making current philosophical expositions of church doctrine seem uninspiring in comparison. Others, struck by the seemingly simple faith of the early Christians, questioned the accumulation of laws, rituals, and hierarchical offices in the church. They found the church's involvement in politics and finance to be abhorrent.

The invention of the printing press, then, was one of the factors that brought about the fragmentation of Western Christianity into the Roman Catholic and numerous Protestant and Reformed Churches. The rulers of nations and regions defined themselves as champions of particular Christian denominations. Bloody religious wars and persecutions erupted. All the denominations tended to define themselves over and against one other. This oppositional identity influenced their practices and beliefs.[75] In their various communities, many Protestants tended toward congregational governance and emphasized the authority of the Bible. Catholics responded by strengthening centralized, hierarchical authority and stressing the liturgical and sacramental life of the community.

## 16. The Modern Period

Other innovations produced further effects. The inventions of the compass, sextant, and clock made navigation over great distances possible. In combination, these devices permitted sailors to calculate their location even when far removed from land. An era of exploration and discovery began. New routes around Africa to the Far East were found, expanding trade and commerce even further. A "new world" was discovered across the great ocean-sea and the various European nations competed with one another to establish colonies and find riches there. New trading commodities and routes were established. New foods began to augment the European diet. Optimism for the future was high. Enormous missionary movements were initiated by the various Christian denominations.

These developments brought out the best and the worst of European Christian culture. Greed and arrogance gave rise to the horrors of the African slave trade and the ill treatment of the native peoples in the new world. Christian belief that all human beings were made in God's image and were descended from common parents clashed with an ancient penchant for dismissing non-Christians as damned. Some found it all too easy, when it was personally advantageous, to emphasize the heathen or even sub-human status of subjugated peoples. Unaware of the existence of microscopic germs that decimated the native populations who had no resistance to European diseases, such people saw the collapse of indigenous nations as evidence that God wanted Europeans to triumph. Others heroically defended their fellow human beings. Moved by ethical concerns, some undertook to introduce the new peoples to the love of God through acts of genuine charity and solidarity. Others who had experienced persecution themselves during European religious wars sought to establish new societies in which everyone could be an equal participant. Victims of religious intolerance hoped to discover refuge in the colonies founded on such principles. These searchers included Jews, who by this time in some European cities were being confined to locked neighborhoods called ghettoes.

In this period of "enlightenment" new political and philosophical ideas arose. The notion of inalienable human rights, bestowed by the Creator on each person, became popular in the West. Governments and rulers had to respect these rights and freedoms or else the people could legitimately replace them. Democratic and republican political theories abounded. These ideas were the under-pinnings of both the American and French Revolutions, which, in turn, encouraged the development of democratic forms of govern-ment in the West. Protestant churches, many of which were organ-ized along local, congregational lines, were generally in accord with these governmental developments, although in some colonies full rights were denied to Catholics, Jews, and others. Some Roman Catholic leaders had become accustomed to a society arranged in class levels and were comfortable with the medieval notion of a "divine right of kings" in which monarchs were held to govern at God's appointment, and not by the consent of their subjects. The chaos of the French Revolution only encouraged their alarm over the decline of monarchical and aristocratic authority and their suspi-cions of the growing power of the masses.

With the rise of secular democracies, Jews had the opportu-nity to escape from their walled life within the ghetto. Many entered into commercial and professional careers and made sig-nificant contributions in the sciences and the arts in the nations where they dwelled. More Jews became assimilated into the majority European society since the days of the Roman Empire. Some Jews felt that Judaism itself needed to adapt to the changing circumstances of the modern world. The Reform movement began as an effort to "modernize" Jewish practice. Jews who resisted such innovations called themselves the Orthodox. The Conservative movement arose as a middle ground between Orthodoxy and Reform. A later Reconstructionist movement would stress Judaism's adaptability to changing circumstances and relativize the authority of traditional practice and teaching.

Although religious intolerance was deemed outdated in enlightened society, bigotry against Jews persisted nonetheless. It became most evident when some assimilated Jews continued to observe their own customs and religious practices. The prominence of Jews in certain professions and in finance contributed to resent-ments against them. Their emancipation from the ghettoes brought new prosperity, but also new perils, to European Jews. In response to the widely publicized exposé of the conviction of a French Jewish army officer on the basis of forged evidence, some Jewish leaders feared that their people could never be safe except in a country of their own. Acting upon a deeply felt yearning for the land of Israel, these leaders began a movement called Zionism that sought to establish a Jewish homeland in Palestine. The Zionists met with cool receptions from many of the governments from which they sought support and from the pope as well.

Meanwhile, many important scientific, economic, and political changes had been taking place. The industrial revolution had caused major population shifts as people left rural areas and poured into cities seeking jobs in the growing number of factories. The mass production of goods made useful items widely available, but it also promoted protracted hours of hazardous working conditions for men, women, and even young children. Eventually, unions of laborers came together to pressure employers for just working conditions. Sometimes violent confrontations between ownership and labor erupted. Churches at first suspected but later supported these labor rights movements.

These social conflicts helped produce a theory of political dynamics known as socialism. This political philosophy viewed human societies in terms of class struggles between elite aristocracies and the masses of working people. Socialist movements arose throughout the Western world, advocating justice for the common folk and the sharing of resources among all the people. A related philosophy, communism, thought this could best be accomplished by the abolition of private property rights. The state would own everything and see to a fair distribution among its population. This social form was opposed to the prevailing capitalist structure that was based upon personal rights and freedoms, commercial competition, and free enterprise. Jews and Christians were represented in all these movements. Different nations experimented with these varying political forms. Civil wars and international conflicts broke out that were partially caused by these rival philosophies of government.

The rise of psychology brought new ways of thinking about the human person. People were understood as possessing a unique, individual consciousness that was shaped by personal experiences and environment. One's inner mental states could influence personal behavior without the conscious knowledge of the person. An awareness of the unique subjectivity of each human being, and of the distinctive perspectives resulting from gender, ethnicity, or socio-economic class, became common in Western nations.

This influenced the contemporary understanding of history. People living in the past were recognized as having been shaped by their cultural presuppositions and environment. They were just as subjectively formed by their historical contexts as were people alive today. With this historical consciousness, it became evident that modern readers had to attempt to immerse themselves in the cultures and worlds of the writers of the past if they hoped truly to comprehend the literature of long ago.

The appearance of evolutionary approaches to reality also had a tremendous impact on Western society. This outlook perceived that the universe, the planet earth, and life itself did not pop into existence fully formed, but rather developed over epochal periods of time. While the exact mechanisms that promoted gradual or sudden changes in these diverse processes of formation were not entirely clear, over the decades scientific evidence mounted and converged in support of the evolutionary perspective. This caused tremendous controversy throughout society, especially when the origins of the human species were under discussion. A static view of reality had prevailed for millennia, making process approaches seem unstable and unsettling. Evolutionary theories were also seen as denying the existence of a creator God. Some researchers actually did make such theological assertions, but evolutionary science in and of itself could not empirically validate such claims. Certain Christian religious bodies were for many years highly suspicious of or actively opposed to evolutionary approaches. Some still are today. Internationally, organized Christian denominations, such as the Roman Catholic Church, have since concluded that evolutionary processes have been substantially demonstrated and theologies incorporating evolutionary ideas have developed in their communities.[76] Some Christian groups developed statements of fundamental principles in opposition both to evolutionary ideas and to the application of the historical consciousness to biblical texts.

One negative consequence of evolutionary theories was how they were used to support racist ideas. Some people simplistically applied the evolutionary concept of the "survival of the fittest" to human beings, both as individuals and as arbitrarily defined racial groups. They argued that people with allegedly inferior intelligence or physical or emotional disorders should not be permitted to have children. They arranged racial groups in a hierarchy of inferiority and superiority. White, northern Europeans were self-servingly deemed to be the most advanced race, destined by their advanced capabilities to dominate all other peoples. This ideology was used to justify stereotypes or to explain the subjugation of African peoples, the alleged untrustworthiness of Asian peoples, and the supposed corruptive influence of Jews. Racial anti-Semitism heightened antipathy toward Jews who were already held in suspicion in Western culture because of medieval Christendom's anti-Jewish theology and practices.

All of these changes in terms of technology, government, industry, and human self-understanding occurred at an ever-accelerating pace. Feelings of instability and disequilibrium grew. Political and economic rivalries and crises flared into two global wars in which new technologies of mass destruction obliterated human lives on previously unimaginable scales. Even in local conflicts or in governmental repression within a single nation, millions of people were now being slain.

These two planetary conflicts sparked efforts to bring unity and collaboration among peoples and nations. Within Christianity an ecumenical movement arose. It sought to bring the disparate denominations of Christianity into harmony with one another.

The World Council of Churches was founded in order to pursue this goal. Politically, a League of Nations formed after the First World War to provide a forum for settling international disputes. Its successor after the Second World War, the United Nations, continues that mission and is also concerned with human rights, education, and the abolition of poverty among all people.

The second of the two global wars produced the greatest devastation the world had yet seen. It confronted the Jewish people with the worst calamity in their long history. In a genocide in which all the destructive capabilities of the modern world seem to have come together, three-fourths of all the Jews in Europe were exterminated. With mechanical brutality and inhuman science, the Nazi regime in Germany oversaw the construction and operation of factories of death that efficiently tortured, slaughtered, and disposed of the corpses of six million Jews. One-and-a-half million Jewish children perished in the annihilation. Although great numbers of other people also died at Nazi hands, Jews especially were hunted down and eradicated because of their mere existence.[77] Humankind's capacity for sin seems to have reached an unbelievable crescendo as other genocides have also occurred in the bloodiest of all human centuries.

The fact that the *Shoah* occurred in the heart of Christian Europe generated devastating questions: Where was God? Of what benefit was it to be in covenant with a God who did not save the dying children? Did the general Christian failure to combat the Nazis, and even the widespread support of the Third Reich among numerous Christians, reveal a religion based upon hatred for Jews? To what extent was historical Christian anti-Jewish teaching to blame for the abomination? Did religion have any purpose in a world insanely destroying itself with recurrent genocide, nuclear homicide, and environmental suicide?[78]

## 17. *Covenanting Life in the World Today*

The disasters of the twentieth century led some, including some Jews and Christians, to the conclusion that God was dead, if indeed God had ever lived. But the long story of Jews and Christians had shown repeatedly that after catastrophe comes rebirth and renewal. For Jews this had occurred after the destruction of both the first and second temples and the periodic expulsions from various countries. In all of these cases, tremendous creativity and rebuilding came to pass. Christians saw the same covenantal pattern in the crucifixion and exaltation of Jesus Christ, the Christianizing of the Roman Empire after decades of persecution, and the rebirths that followed the collapses and transgressions over the centuries. And so, even with the twentieth century's shattering cataclysms, signs of renewal and promise could be detected.

These renewals challenged both Jews and Christians to reengage history with purpose and conviction. For many Jews, the foundation of the state of Israel was a defining triumph. All their people could now find a homeland there. The just governance of a diverse population in which Jews were the majority, however, brought challenges for which Jews had little historical preparation. Their experiences for millennia had been as a tolerated or oppressed minority. At its worst, this context encouraged and coerced a withdrawal from history into the ghetto. The Torah vision of a society of justice and peace could be attempted only internally within narrow horizons. The existence of a Jewish state, especially one dominating hundreds of thousands of indigenous Arab peoples, brought about the urgent demand for the pursuit of the Torah's justice and peace in extremely complex political and religious circumstances. This task was rendered even more difficult by a "cold war" of superpower ideological competition that fostered regional violence and hostility. Tremendous ethical challenges accompany the Jewish renewal in *Eretz Yisrael,* the Land of Israel.

The Jewish reemergence onto the historical stage also brought challenges in terms of Jewish identity. The various modern Jewish movements, Reform, Reconstructionist, Conservative, and Orthodox, with all their internal diversities, have yet to settle their own interrelationships, especially in Israel. The appearance of a significant population of so-called "secular" Jews also raises questions about Jewish self-definition. In the diaspora, a high rate of intermarriage with non-Jews is a further challenge. In some ways, the situation for Jews today recalls the wide-ranging variety of the late second temple period. In addition, Jews are now being confronted with major changes in Christian attitudes toward Judaism.

In different ways, the previous few centuries had encouraged Christians to withdraw from history to some degree as well. The rise of secular democracies with the consequent decline in ecclesial power, the divisions with the church itself, the radical and rapid changes brought about by the scientific and industrial revolutions, and the devastation wrought by famines, wars, and genocides—all could contribute to a spirituality that focused on the individual Christian living a good life so as to escape from the sinful world into the happiness of heaven. In the Roman Catholic, but also in other churches, there was a powerful impetus to shut out the prevailing culture behind defensive walls of religious certainty that rejected the fallen world.

However, the forces that promoted a Christian fortress mentality beckoned other Christians to incarnate their covenant with God by engaging the contemporary world and culture. The Roman Catholic Church prominently manifested this in convening the Second Vatican Council. For the first time, Catholic bishops from around the entire world gathered together to discuss and debate the mission of the church in the contemporary world. Their four years of deliberations brought about powerful renewals in the Catholic Church's self-understanding. The Catholic Church, the council declared, has a mission to ready the world for the coming of God's Kingdom by promoting the inestimable value of the human being, by working in modern society to promote justice and peace as yeast leavens the dough, by vitalizing its own sacramental and liturgical life to empower its members in their mission, and by reaching out with respect and esteem to other Christians and to non-Christians to collaborate in the work of enhancing human life. Far from fleeing from history into a heavenly afterlife, the council taught that the church has a responsibility to permeate human societies with the values of God's Kingdom. It has an obligation to seek to turn humanity from sinful self-destruction to the life of enabling relationship that images God.

The effects of the Second Vatican Council continue to be tremendous. Although some have rejected its reforms and resisted its renewal, Catholics in particular and Christians in general will be pursuing its lofty vision for many, many years into the new millennium.

One of the council's most dramatic changes concerned the Catholic Church's relationship with the Jewish people. It declared that Jews remained beloved of God and could not be held culpable for the death of Jesus, thereby repudiating standard Christian understandings since the days of the Roman Empire.[79] The council's statement prompted the composition of numerous other Christian documents concerning Christian-Jewish relations, both within the Catholic Church and among a wide range of other Christian denominations.

The church today recognizes that the Jewish people continue to dwell in a perpetual covenantal bonding with God. It also acknowledges that Jews have an ongoing divine vocation in the world that can only be articulated by Jews themselves. These realizations challenge Christians to revise theologies and practices that had been based on the presupposition of Israel's obsolescence and replacement. Since so much of Christian self-understanding was previously defined in opposition to Judaism, the reversal of its negative attitudes will also have an unfolding impact on Christian self-identity.

In the years ahead, this renewal in Christian sentiments toward Judaism will also challenge Jews. The habit of building barriers against a traditionally demeaning majority religion will hopefully become obsolete when confronted by an affirming and supportive church. Jews will experience the unfamiliar situation of needing to respond theologically to a renewed Christianity that addresses Jews as siblings and teaches that God desires Jews and Christians to collaborate.

Indeed, it could be said that the end of the second millennium of the Christian story is remarkably exceptional because it is witnessing the first really intensive reflection on the mystery of the relationship between the church and Judaism. Christian and Jewish thinkers are wondering if God intends Jews and Christians to need each other's help in fulfilling their covenantal mission. Some have wondered if Christians stress that God seeks relationship with the individual, an emphasis that Israel balances with a focus on God's communal summons.[80] Some have speculated that Christians need Jewish reminders that the Reign of God has not yet arrived, while Jews need the Christian awareness that in some ways the Reign has already begun.[81] Some have conjectured that Jews are a constant admonition to Christians of the dangers of triumphalism, while Christians summon Jews to avoid the seductions of introspective insularity.[82] Many participants in Jewish-Christian dialogue feel that both communities need one another to overcome the burdens of their history together.[83] Pope John Paul II has said that God desires Jews and Christians to be a blessing for the world[84] and has formally committed the Catholic Church to "genuine brotherhood with the people of the Covenant."[85]

A third millennium for Christians thus begins with the church and Judaism both on the threshold of a profound renewal. The account of their journey together could be transformed from a tale of contention into a story of *shalom*. The Hebrew tradition, forebearer of both Jews and Christians, understood *shalom* to be the peace and wholeness that is the fruit of right relationship. For nearly a score of centuries, Christians and Jews have not lived in a right relationship with one another. Although both share life with God covenantally, their histories show that they have not experienced the mutual wholeness that should accompany their covenantal existence. Now there are unprecedented opportunities to aspire to the *shalom* that should flourish between us. We may experience a new and extended period of covenantal renewal.

Such a development would be a force for hope in a world beset by challenges.[86] New awareness of the complexities and unpredictability of reality has infused our postmodern world with widespread uncertainties. Technological revolutions accelerate. Intricate ethical questions arise with genetic research and experimentation. Environmental degradation, the decline in global biodiversity, and climatic alterations remain troublesome threats. Human dignity is jeopardized in previously unimaginable ways.

The future holds great potential as well as great challenges. Instantaneous global communications can serve to bring humanity together to aid victims of natural disasters or injustice. It can also promote education throughout the entire human family and so lift the human species from the darkness of ignorance. Genetic research can assist in curing numerous diseases and in promoting worldwide biodiversity. Growing knowledge of the interactive complexities of the planetary ecosystem can give humanity the necessary tools to be true stewards of creation thereby living up to the responsibilities that sentience bestows.

Jews and Christians live in a covenanting relationship with God that requires us to confront these challenges and pursue these prospects with a divine vision. Sharing life with God in communities of faith, we have a common understanding of God's intentions for the world. In our pain we experience the sinfulness and incompleteness of creation and know that our divine Covenant Partner expects us to be involved in its healing and fulfillment. We perceive, and must ourselves resist, the sinful forces in the world that encourage people to be inhuman and unlike God. Instead, we must consciously foster those developments that enrich life. Indeed, as time passes, God may be expecting more and more of human covenanting partners.[87]

Christians and Jews experience in both similar and distinctive ways God's presence reaching out to us, enabling us to assume our covenantal mission. For Jews, Sabbath observances and other traditional practices are anticipatory experiences of the Age to Come that serve to refocus their vision and mission anew. For Christians, the Eucharist is a covenant renewal ceremony in which we recommit ourselves to Jesus' mission of preparing God's Reign. God is always there—sustaining us, extending covenanting relationship and mission, and empowering our participation in that relationship and mission. Truly we are both People of the Covenant.

Through word, ritual, education, and action, Jews and Christians both live out our common mission as servants of the Reign of God in the circumstances of our time. We pass on this mission to our children. Today we have been graced with the realization that we are meant to pursue our mission in collaboration with others. We are required to do this in gratitude to the God who created and sustains us, who calls and empowers us. We are to be partners with God and with one another in doing the justice and love and mercy that will pervade God's Reign of *shalom.*

God, who is relational and generous, has graced us with the choice to cooperate in a great, ennobling, and redemptive task. As we Christians begin the third millennium of our life as a covenanting community, we must approach this mission with awe and humility and dependence on the One who has called us. Our story thus far has had its triumphs, and also its infidelities and horrors. Our task for the foreseeable future involves healing, with God's help, the divisions that afflict our little world. Our petty conflicts are not meant to be the defining feature of human existence. Our disputes are, after all, quite insignificant from the perspective of a vast universe, the immensity of which staggers our feeble imaginations. Paradoxically and astonishingly, the God who sustains all existence constantly invites us to help bring about a universe in which ultimately "God will be all in all" (1 Cor 15:28).

# Postlude:
# Theologies That Promote Shalom

As indicated in the prelude, this retelling of the Christian story makes a number of theological decisions and narrative moves. This essay briefly sketches the major perspectives that were incorporated. Obviously, entire volumes could be composed about each of them. These are provided to offer stimuli for further reflection.

## 1. Divine Revelation Occurs Through Our Relationships with God in Time

Based on the biblical witness and on a historically conscious approach to reality, the story just told was premised on the conviction that all human encounters with God are mediated through life's experiences in the created world (as noted in the prelude) and are also essentially relational.

To say that human encounters with God are relational means that humans must *respond* to the myriad historical mediations of God's presence and actions in order for revelations to occur. A subjective, human decision to interpret particular, concrete experiences as disclosive of the divine is required.[88] Different people can witness or experience the same events or series of occurrences, but only some of them might conclude that God's activity has been revealed. Not everyone who participated in or witnessed

63

the escape from Egypt of forced laborers would conclude that God had chosen these people for special purposes; neither would everyone who observed an empty tomb judge that a corpse had been transformed to new life.[89] Sometimes a revelation occurs only with hindsight, when sufficient time has passed for reflection on the true nature of certain experiences to be discerned and acknowledged.

These dynamics may reflect God's profound respect for the divine gift of free will to humanity. Dramatic displays of divine power would be coercive. They would overwhelm human capacities to choose freely. Both Israel and the church experience God as one who does not use force or might to subjugate human beings. Instead, God subtly and ambiguously calls out to people. In this way they must freely choose whether to respond.[90]

Recognition of the relational nature of revelation raises the possibility that such disclosures are divinely aimed or targeted. Not only must divine self-disclosure be mediated through the created world—because of the limitations of time-bound mortals— but it is conceivable that God selects the recipients of particular disclosures. The appearance narratives in the gospels might illustrate this. With one famous exception, the Crucified and Raised One is only manifested to people who already were his disciples. Persons such as Pontius Pilate or Caiaphas, for instance, do not encounter the transcendent Jesus. Relationship with the Crucified One seems to have facilitated the revelation of him as raised. On the other hand, God may select for a certain revelation people without such prior relationships, Paul of Tarsus being the noteworthy example.

Thus, a relational understanding of revelation offers a further explanation of why a certain specific event makes God known to some people and not to others. Not only must the human participants choose to respond to God's invitation, but God must also have extended the particular self-disclosure in that specific setting in the first place. However, given our limited perceptions, it is impossible for human beings to judge what combination of divine and human intentions permitted or prevented a revelation from occurring to specific people through a certain event or particular situation.

In *any* relational self-disclosure of the divine, the triune God is always at work. The One who sustains creation delicately invites people to relationship, while at the same time enabling them to choose to perceive and to accept the invitation. These continuous and simultaneous divine movements permeate processes of revelation. All created reality may serve as instruments of God's activity. This includes natural beauty, seasonal changes, living things, and perhaps most especially, human interactions: the camaraderie of friends, the touch of a spouse, the smile of a son or daughter. Christians understand that God's invitation to relationship was revealed most powerfully and palpably in the life and death of the Galilean Jew, Jesus, and continues to be dynamically extended today through the church, the historical body of that Living Crucified and Raised One.

The human partners to a revelatory process are driven to communicate their experience to others. Again, the first preachers of Jesus as raised illustrate this. Through their agency, relationship to God through Christ was spread to others who had never had direct personal contact with Jesus the Galilean. However, due to the subjective quality of human encounters with divine self-disclosure, such transcendent experiences are invariably difficult to convey to other people. Metaphors and symbols are by nature capable of sustaining both the multidimensionality and ambiguity of divine self-disclosure, and so are very frequently used to attempt to impart revelatory experiences. They may indeed be the most powerful human means to describe human meetings with the divine in human history. (This is a major reason why the medium of a theological narrative, a story, has been chosen to express the Christian legacy in this volume.)

Once more, the gospel resurrection accounts illustrate this very well, though many other biblical examples could be adduced. When the evangelists described the earliest perceptions that the crucified Jesus was transcendently alive, they used "appearance" narratives. Confusion and lack of recognition by Jesus' friends and a lack of consistency in terms of settings, timings, and characters typify these narratives.[91] The power of this relational revelatory event was such that efforts to conceptualize it and express it in human speech were inevitably difficult. The same holds true in varying degrees for other human interactions with the divine. Nonetheless, the creative energy unleashed by such revelatory encounters with God has generated texts of transcendent power that invite readers into encounters with God through the mediation of the written word.

## 2. *We Interpret the Bible by Dialoguing with It*

This leads to a brief description of the biblical hermeneutical principles that underlie this work. In Catholicism today biblical interpretation is understood as essentially a dialogical process. It is a conversation between faith communities of today and their ancestors in faith about their experiences of God.[92]

In this conversational process, two distinct activities must occur: explanation and understanding. Explanation utilizes all the historical and literary critical tools at our disposal to seek to describe the intended meaning of the scriptural text. Understanding examines our own questions, presuppositions, and world in order to comprehend the text's relevance and transformative meaning for us today. Another way to put this is that understanding seeks to "actualize," to bring the text to life, in our very different cultural and historical contexts.[93]

This process of actualizing ancient texts can be seen within the Bible itself. Later authors reinterpreted earlier ones in different circumstances and so actualized their writings in new and creative ways. They found new meanings by bringing new questions and concerns to the text. In the words of the Pontifical Biblical Commission, "later biblical writings often depend upon earlier ones. These more recent writings allude to older ones, [and] create 'rereadings' which develop new aspects of meaning, sometimes quite different from the original sense."[94] To illustrate this point, the commission offered several examples from the Shared Testament. For instance, Jeremiah's reference to Judah's punishment by the Babylonians for seventy years (Jer 25:11–12; 29:10) is considered to have been satisfied in the past by the author of Chronicles (2 Chr 25:20–23), but is thought by the writer of Daniel 9:24–27 to find its true meaning in the struggle with Antiochus IV in his own era.[95] The same process of actualization was at work in the composition of the books of the Christian Testament. By reading the texts of ancient Israel through resurrection lenses, Christian writers perceived new meanings in the ancient texts, especially those of the prophets and psalms.

In this retelling of the Christian story, the developmental understanding of the biblical witness was respected. This historically based narrative attempted to sketch out the historical bases for the foundational revelatory moments of Judaism and Christianity, but also noted the different oral and literary traditions that arose when further implications of the foundational revelations became apparent in later historical circumstances.

In a related fashion, the retold story historically sketched the Christian tradition from postbiblical times to the present as continuous actualizations of the Christian message in varying historical periods. This led to the present moment and the efforts of contemporary generations to incarnate and implement the Christian mission in our own context.

## 3. *Christ Embodies Covenanting Life*

The christological aspects of this story incorporated the biblical and historical principles described just above and in the introduction. Christ was not introduced ontologically, but rather as historically experienced by his Jewish contemporaries, by his disciples, and after his death by the apostles. The christological approach utilized in the narrative of the story could loosely be called a "covenantal christology" because it apprehends the significance of Jesus Christ through a relational metaphysic.

By beginning a christology with the life and death of the Galilean Jew, Jesus of Nazareth, one typically encounters the problem of how to introduce his divine status as the incarnate *Logos,* or Word of God. On the other hand, starting a christology with the preexistent *Logos* often leads to difficulty in maintaining Jesus' authentic humanity. It seems likely that the dichotomous categories utilized in patristic ontological christologies lie at the root of these difficulties.

An approach grounded on the historical mediation of the divine and on a relational metaphysic can help avoid such problems by using different thought categories. Since the church, as Pope John Paul II has observed, does not "canonize any one particular philosophy in preference to others,"[96] there is no reason in principle why this should not be tried.

Thus, this telling of the Christian story first presented Jesus historically as a Galilean Jew who undertook a mission of preparing his people Israel for the imminent commencement of the Reign of God. His historical ministry was characterized theologically as the tangible manifestation of the life of the Age to Come. After his death at the hands of the Roman occupiers and their pawns, his followers experienced a revelation. They were enabled by God to perceive that the Crucified One had been raised to transcendent new life. He was living and manifesting the new life of the Age to Come. This conviction was not something that could be demonstrated empirically, because the concrete evidence of the empty tomb could be variously interpreted. Once having affirmed this revelation, however, his apostles were enabled to comprehend that they were experiencing God's continuous invitation to relationship through the Crucified and Raised One. They had met God in history in a human being who was simultaneously the divine *Logos.* If the *Logos* is conceived relationally as divine invitation to covenanting relationship, then one might say that in

Jesus the Galilean his contemporaries experienced covenanting personified—the very life of the triune God.

This is suggested by the mutual indwelling *(perichoresis)* language of the Gospel of John, which portrays the Father, Son, and Spirit "abiding in" one another. In Johannine thinking, believers perceive that Jesus and the Father are "in" each other (John 14:11). Consequently, the love that the Father has for Jesus comes into believers (17:26). The Father and the Son (14:23) and the Spirit (14:17) come to dwell in believers. Thus, believers live according to Jesus' only commandment in this gospel, "Love one another" (13:34; 15:12,17). This is what John means by eternal life. It is a sharing in the love-relationship between the Father and the Son in the Spirit. It is a love/life that transcends human death. It is a relationship with the Father made possible because the Son came down from above and has returned to his home above "to prepare a place" and take believers there (14:3). Using the language of covenant in an ontological way, a Christian can say that Jesus' divinity brings into history the very covenanting life of the Trinity, a covenanting way of living entered into by Israel and perfectly lived out in Jesus' humanity.

That is why this postsupersessionist telling of the Christian story likewise understands Jesus, the faithful son of Israel, as embodying and fulfilling (in the sense of living out in its fullest intensity) Israel's covenanting life with God. He epitomized what life in covenant was and is all about. This means that Israel's covenanting life with God must be permanent and vital since the church knows with certainty that its covenanting with God through Christ is permanent and vital. If Israel's covenanting is deemed to be obsolete or inert, then Jesus would be mediating and inviting the church to a relationship with God that is also possibly temporary, obsolete, or inert. This is unthinkable. It would be contrary to the character of the triune God to establish a covenantal bonding that was not founded upon divine fidelity and empowerment.[97] A christology that understands Jesus as epitomizing and mediating Israel's covenanting life, then, must inevitably affirm the "covenant of eternal love which was never revoked"[98] between God and the Jewish people.

Conceiving of Jesus as the embodiment of Israel's covenaning history is suggested by two Christian Testament sources. In the Gospel of Matthew, Jesus is seen as a reprise and culmination of preceding Jewish history. For example, the infancy narrative contains a tripartite genealogy (1:1–17) featuring four notable women whose stories anticipate Jesus' unusual birth (1:3,5,6); a number of "fulfillment" passages that relate Jesus to prophetic texts (1:22–23; 2:5–6,14–15,17–18,23); and allusions to famous Hebrews of the past, for example, Joseph, who like his biblical forebear, receives dream-messages (1:20; 2:13,19,22); and Moses, who like Jesus, was rescued as an infant from a murderous king (2:16–18). Likewise, Jesus' ministry begins with three temptations in the desert that correspond to the experiences of Israel in the desert after the exodus, but where Israel son of God failed, Jesus Son of God succeeds (compare Exod 16:1–3; 17:1–2,7; 32:1–4 with Matt 4:3–10). He is, in effect, the perfect son of Israel, the perfect Jew. For the Apostle Paul, Jesus was the perfect human, the perfect Adam. As messiah-king, he epitomizes and represents Israel.[99]

Jesus walked God's way with perfect fidelity and, like Israel, he suffered for his faithfulness to God. Like Israel, he also experienced a divine covenantal restoration after his suffering, though in a unique transhistorical way, by being raised up. His transcendent life shows that death itself will be defeated in the inevitable Reign of God.

As the unique human incarnation of divine outreach (the *Logos,* or Son of God) and the embodiment of perfect human covenanting with God (son of Israel), Jesus Christ, the Crucified and Raised One, unites in himself the human and divine existences that partner in covenanting. The Christian experience of relationship with God is therefore christomorphic. It is shaped and defined by the ongoing mediation of Christ. It is also universal in that it understands that what God has done in Christ will ultimately bring all humanity into covenanting life with God so the creation itself may be fully achieved (see, e.g., 1 Cor 15:28, Rom 8:18–25).

It is precisely because Jesus Christ embodies covenanting life that "[h]e who encounters Jesus Christ encounters Judaism."[100] It is *Israel's* covenanting life that the human Jesus of Nazareth personifies. It is the God irrevocably linked in covenant with Israel whose constant divine outreach for relationship is made present in Jesus. To forget this is "...to detach [Christ] from his roots and to empty his mystery of all meaning."[101]

But how is Christ to be related to Israel's historically earlier revelatory experiences of God? The recent declaration of the Congregation for the Doctrine of the Faith, *Dominus Iesus,* while combating attitudes of religious relativism, skirts but does not directly address this question. Clearly, supersessionist "approaches that reduce [the Hebrew Scriptures] to a propadeutic or background for the New Testament"[102] are inadequate in a church that rejoices in "the unfathomable riches of the Old Testament...[which] retains its own value as revelation that the New Testament often does no more than resume"[103] and that also urges Christians "to learn by what essential traits Jews define themselves in the light of their own religious experience."[104]

My own effort to address this question is connected to the way that the terms *Logos* and *Christ* have been employed in this work. *Logos* has been used to name what is ontologically called the "Second Person of the Blessed Trinity" and what I have attempted to call relationally (and dynamically) the constant divine invitation to relationship with God. The "Word" God speaks is not simply information. It is a personal beckoning.

*Christ* has been described herein as the church's way of naming its recognition that the Crucified and Raised One is none other than Jesus of Galilee, that he incarnated the *Logos* while living on earth and that the *Logos* now is united with a transcendently exalted Jew.

In other words, from our limited vantage point in linear time the eternal *Logos,* God's constant invitation to covenantal relationship, cannot *historically* be equated with Christ until after the life, death, and resurrection of Jesus of Galilee. For Christians who have experienced a covenantal revelation of the Crucified and Raised One as God's divine call, the *Logos* and Christ are now recognized to be coextensive terms. Somehow, all of God's divine activity throughout the created universe, activity that transcends the limits of our imagination and vision, now intrinsically involves a certain exalted Jew.

The subtle distinction I am advancing here does not violate the injunction of *Dominus Iesus* against introducing "any sort of separation between the Word and Jesus Christ [as] contrary to the Christian faith."[105] Operating from within the constraints of linear time and the historically mediated and relational nature of revelation, I am pointing out that *temporally,* looking out from within historical time, the *"Logos"* was not "Christ" until after the incarnation and no human being experienced such a revelation until after the resurrection. *Dominus Iesus* indeed implicitly acknowledges this, even though it is not addressing questions of Jewish-Christian relations, when it states, "[T]he theory which would attribute, after the incarnation as well, a salvific activity to the Logos as such in his divinity, exercised 'in addition to' or 'beyond' the humanity of Christ, is not compatible with the Catholic faith."[106] Apparently, and presumably unavoidably, the situation is different *before* the incarnation. Then the divine activity of the *Logos* had to be "beyond" the humanity of Christ since the human Jesus of Galilee had yet to be born. Subsequently, however, "[w]ith the incarnation, all the salvific actions of the Word of God are always done in unity with the human nature that he has assumed for the salvation of all people."[107] This last comment raises profound theological prospects since the human nature in question belonged to a Jewish human being. The covenantal bonding between God and Israel assumed a new intimacy with the birth of Jesus and this intimacy has cosmic consequences.

How does all this help with the question of how Jesus Christ is to be related to Israel's historically earlier revelatory experiences of God? All Christians believe that what I prefer to call the Shared Testament was composed under divine inspiration. That inspiration was given through the grace of the Triune One—sustaining, inviting, and empowering. The covenanting life expressed and guided by the *Tanakh* is that same way of living with a relational God that later historically came to human life in Jesus of Galilee.

In the Christian Bible, therefore, the Shared Testament and the Christian Testament reciprocally reinforce one another because both are articulations of the *Logos* of covenanting life. The Shared Testament testifies to Israel's millennium-long experience of a covenanting God and the Christian Testament bears witness to the apostles' experience of the same covenanting God in Christ. This is also why Catholic documents constantly reiterate that the church and the Jewish people are spiritually linked—both have responded to the *Logos'* divine invitation to covenant.[108] The relationship of Jesus Christ to Israel's witness is one of fulfillment, not in the sense of replacing or terminating, but in the sense of confirming, supporting, and furthering.[109]

This conception of "fulfillment" has significance for one's understanding of *messiah* and *messianism.* In recent decades, scholars have rediscovered the vast diversity of Jewish messianic expectations in the late second temple period. There did not exist one universally acknowledged messianic template with which Jesus of Nazareth could simply be compared. After experiencing him as transcendently raised, the apostles indeed understood him as Israel's messiah, but in ways that no Jew had previously imagined. The radical novelty of Christian postresurrectional messianic understandings is conveyed in this account by using the Greek term *Christ* to refer to the church's experience of God in the Crucified and Raised One. The fact that this term quickly became a name rather than a title for the raised Jesus shows how inadequately the term *messiah* expressed the apostles' experiences of their glorified master.

In terms of the eschatological future, this narrative says little about the "messianic age" in which the Reign of God will be fully achieved. The precise scenario or series of events leading to the completion of God's creation is simply unknown to us. That ultimate fulfillment lies in the future.

However, the christology presented in this story does have a certain eschatological direction. While recognizing that "salvation and liberation are already accomplished in Christ,"[110] it highlights the reality that we still await the final establishment of that Kingdom of God for which Jesus lived, died, and was raised. In some ways both Israel's exodus and the birth of the church are "intermediate stages" in the ultimate fulfillment of God's designs.[111]

This christological perspective lends itself to the postsupersessionist goal of Jewish and Christian collaboration, as the 1986 Vatican "Notes" observed:

> [I]n underlining the [futurist] eschatological dimension of Christianity we shall reach a greater awareness that the people of God of the Old and New Testament are tending towards a like end in the future: the coming or the return of the Messiah—even if they start from two different points of view....Attentive to the same God who has spoken, hanging on the same word, we have to witness to one same memory and one common hope in [the One] who is the master of history. We must also accept our responsibility to prepare the world for the coming of the Messiah by working together for social justice, respect for the rights of persons and nations, and for social and international reconciliation. To this we are driven, Jews and Christians, by the command to love our neighbor, by a common hope for the Kingdom of God, and by the great heritage of the Prophets.[112]

Thus, a christology that balances the realized and unrealized aspects of the "Christ-event" leads to a more Kingdom-centered, or basileo-centric, understanding of the church, and a view of salvation as an unfolding task in which the People of the Covenant participate in relationship with God.

## 4. Salvation Is Covenanting Participation in God's Unfolding Plans for Creation

One of the issues that has arisen in postsupersessionist theological reflections is whether to conceive of the covenanting character of Christianity and Judaism in terms of a single covenant with different modalities or as two distinct, parallel covenants.[113] The tensions between the two approaches are partially based on concerns that, on the one hand, a single covenant model runs the constant risk of sliding into Christian supersessionism. On the other hand, a dual covenant model seems to dilute the universal salvific significance of Jesus Christ.

In this telling of the Christian story, care has been taken not to discuss *covenant* simplistically as a contract, an agreement, or an object. Covenant is better comprehended as a continuing action, as "covenanting." Covenanting is an ongoing sharing-in-life between God and human partners. It is not a thing that can simply be bestowed or transferred. Rather, covenanting is a relationship into which a people enter and which constantly grows and deepens, unless specific individuals choose subsequently to deny the relationship's existence.

Applying this awareness to the single-/dual-model debate, it seems reasonable to conclude that both Jews and Christians are sharing in a similar covenanting life with the One God. They have entered into this way of walking through life by different means—Jews through their historical encounters with God now mediated through the Torah, and Christians by encountering in Christ the embodiment of Israel's covenanting life and of God's divine invitation to relationship—but both are engaged with God in preparing for the Age to Come. Their participation in this divine endeavor helps them identify, and with God's help counter, the corrosive effects of sin, egocentrism, and destructiveness in the world.

This approach, therefore, has affinities with the one-covenant model. However, because of the relational and active understanding of *covenant,* both Jews and Christians are seen to be fully involved in the divine instruction to complete the world. Both are covenanting with God because of the divine outreach for relationship, an invitation sustained and empowered by God, but each covenanting community has its own unique and distinctive traditions and way-of-walking with God. Supersessionism is disallowed in this approach because it requires the ongoing dynamism of Israel's covenanting, since Christians are covenanting with the same God whom they know to be faithful.

Conversely, Christians might wonder if this formulation does not suffer from a critique often leveled at the two-covenant model. Namely, how is the universal salvific significance of Jesus Christ to be maintained in the case of Israel? Or alternatively, of what significance is Christ to Jews?

Such a question can be answered from Jewish perspectives or from Christian ones. Following the principle of the 1974 Vatican "Guidelines," Christians must learn to hear how "Jews define themselves in the light of their own religious experience."[114] It is not up to Christians to dictate to Jews what Christ should mean or not mean to them, especially given the sad history of Christian oppression of Jews. Some Jewish thinkers might simply reply, "Nothing—Jesus means nothing to us except as the stated reason for centuries of persecution and marginalization."

The historical reality of Christian oppression of Jews renders discussion of the potential theological significance of Jesus for Jews delicate and perilous for Jewish and Christian commentators alike. In this regard, Peter von der Osten-Sacken points out the importance of Zechariah's Canticle, in Luke 1:68–75. In this passage, Zechariah is portrayed as singing about his newborn son, John the Baptist, and the soon-to-be-born Jesus. He intones, "[The Lord] has raised up for us a horn for our salvation within the house of David his servant, even as he promised through the mouth of his holy prophets from of old: salvation from our enemies and from the hand of all who hate us...and to grant us that, rescued from the hand of enemies, without fear we might worship him, in holiness and righteousness before him all our days" (Luke 1:69–71,73).

Osten-Sacken points out that since Israel's enemies were Gentiles, Luke seems to hope that in the church Gentiles will become Israel's allies and so enable Jews to worship God without fear. Of course, this is not what happened historically. It is worthwhile to quote Osten-Sacken at length:

> But then if God's oath counts for anything at all and if the Christian church lives from the assurance that the fulfillment has already begun in Jesus Christ, there is surely no other way open to the church than to let the Jewish people sense, from its own specific behavior, through the way it lives, something of the fact that a fractional part of the time might really have come for Israel, "delivered out of the hands of its enemies, to serve him fearlessly in holiness and righteousness." But in fact the history of the way Christian churches have behaved to God's people of Israel has run in so diametrically opposite a direction that, throughout the centuries, the Jewish congregations have been delivered *into* the hand of their (Christian) enemies and have had to serve God in fear and trembling—not because of the behavior of some random gentile nations, but because of the acts of nations specifically "Christian." And if, even then, this service has still been joyful, fearless, and in holiness and righteousness, then it is certainly only in exceptional cases that this has been due to the behavior of Christians. The Jewish no to Jesus Christ, and even more to the church, has therefore been legitimated countless times by the obedient behavior of Jews and the disobedient behavior of Christians. The Christian churches will only be what they are called to be for the people of God, as far as is humanly possible, when they have testified convincingly through their lives

and behavior for just as long a period as they filled the
Jewish people with fear and apprehension, that for Israel
they are a reason not for fear but for fearlessness and perhaps even confidence.[115]

The relevance of these observations for our discussion of
covenanting is as follows. It may be that the salvific significance of Jesus for the Jewish relationship with God has never
been historically manifested because of the early embedding of
anti-Jewish theologies into Christian self-definition and practice. If it is appropriate to understand Jesus Christ as the epitome
of Israel's covenanting life, whose death and resurrection
extends that life out to the Gentile nations through the church,
then his significance for Israel should be straightforward.
Israel's salvific participation in the divine task of readying the
world for the Age to Come had advanced by a quantum leap
with the birth of the Gentile church. Over time, a few billion
Christians ought in principle to have joined a few million Jews
in being lights to the nations.

However, in their two millennia of shared history, Jews and
Christians have been enemies, not allies. Our third millennium
together begins with the hopeful opportunity to change this. Since
there exists this almost eschatological way of imagining how
Jesus Christ could be of saving significance for the Jewish people
within the course of history,[116] it would be misguided to fault postsupersessionist Christian theologies for not positing the universal
salvific importance of Jesus Christ in the habitual supersessionist
way that expected all Jews to become Christians. Indeed, comments by Catholic Church leaders on the ongoing "vocation" of
Jews in the world[117] and on the divine sign of their ongoing history
convey that on this side of the eschaton God does not desire Jews
to become Christians.[118] Beyond the eschaton, we shall have to
wait to see what surprises a God of limitless creativity may have
in store for all of us.

## 5. How Do We Teach the Christian Story?

It seems appropriate to sketch a few educational principles generated by this retelling of the Christian story. Obviously, books could be written about each of them, but these brief statements may be helpful launching points for educators and homilists as they perform their ministries.[119]

First, preachers and teachers might exhibit a certain humility in presenting the Christian faith. Although we are covenanting with God through Christ, the One with whom we are in relationship is far beyond our full comprehension or experience. We must always be mindful of our dependence on our creator and sustainer. Humility also arises when one considers on the scale of cosmic time our small place in the vast universe or our brief existence as a species. While the psalmist perceived that humans are little less than divine (Psalm 8:6), he was also awestruck by God's concern for such seemingly insignificant creatures.

Second, because God so transcends us, we must not present our faith tradition as if we are in possession of all the answers to every conceivable question, even though Catholics believe they have been graced with the "fullness of revelation." Even if it were possible to reveal the totality of God to human mortals, our minds would be unable to cope with such limitlessness. Such a scenario would also overwhelm our freedom of choice and is something that a covenanting God doesn't do. Indeed, part of covenanting is that we must constantly decide how to promote the Age to Come in our particular and ever-changing circumstances. Therefore, our Christian tradition should be presented as a journey with God on which we stumble and grow in response to our call.

Third, we must emphasize that God has intentions for our still incomplete world and that these intentions include human participation in building the world according to God's will. No doubt it is impossible in the present to foresee all of the ways that human beings can advance God's Reign in the future. We must consciously and conscientiously pursue our covenanting responsibilities for all the future opportunities to become clear.

Fourth, when referring to the Jewish people we should always note that their relationship with God is ongoing and perpetual. It is a relationship that bestows on Jews the covenanting obligation to prepare the world for God's Way of reconciliation, justice, peace, and mercy.

Fifth, let us stress Christian baptismal responsibilities. Through baptism, we Christians have undertaken to continue the mission of Jesus Christ. This commitment and duty is renewed each time we share in the Eucharist. Our participation in and dedication to the mission of Christ sweeps us into God's salvific plans for creation.

Sixth, we ought to observe, whenever appropriate, that Israel, Jesus Christ, and the church each are living in the service of the coming Reign of God. Consequently, Christians and Jews are divinely intended to be allies and collaborators in preparing the world for the Age to Come. Despite their violent history, the formation of wholeness and right relationship, of true *shalom,* between Jews and Christians will be a powerful sign to a world in need of reconciliation and healing. It is what the Spirit is leading us toward today.

# Appendix:
# An Outline of *A Story of Shalom*

- This is a story about the past, present, and future of the Christian people and the other People of the Covenant, the Jewish people.

- It occurs on one small planet in a vast and unfinished universe, brought into being and sustained by the one God.

- On this small planet, God slowly brought sentient human beings into existence.

- God subtly invites humans into a divine relationship and empowers them to heed and accept this invitation. God wishes them to cooperate in bringing creation to its fulfillment in an Age to Come of justice, peace, solidarity, mercy, and life.

- God has gifted humans with the capacity to choose to participate in God's designs or to resist and oppose them.

- Over time, human societies became permeated with inducements toward self-centeredness, sin, and violence, contrary to God's intentions. Nonetheless, God continued (and continues) to summon people into divine relationship and into participation in bringing about the Age to Come.

- The people of Israel heard this call in a distinctive way and entered into a covenanting sharing-in-life with God. They became instruments of God's presence in the world. They were summoned to be a light to the world so that God would save and bless humanity.

- The people of Israel knew (and continues to know) God as the one who sustains them, restores them after their own failures and after attacks from others, and empowers them in their mission to ready the world for the Age to Come.

- Jesus of Galilee epitomized Israel's covenanting life and mission. He lived for the Age to Come and made it powerfully present. He also died for the Age to Come, being killed by injustice and sin. Slain by the dominant empire of the nations, he was covenantally restored and transcendently exalted. He was relationally revealed as the human embodiment of God's divine invitation to relationship whose deeds would bring the Reign of God into being and so save all humanity.

- Some Jews, and later many Gentiles, experienced relationship with God through Jesus Christ. They came together in the newly assembled church. They were sustained and empowered to continue Jesus' mission of readying the world for the Age to Come. They learned that sin, injustice, and death itself would come to an end in that coming age.

- The church's relationship with God is thus christomorphic. It is shaped by the continuing Christian experience of the Crucified and Raised One. Moreover, in Jesus Christ, Israel's role to bring the light of the knowledge of God to the world has achieved a historic realization.

- Most Jews did not share in the revelation of Christ crucified and raised. They feared that the new church was disregarding Jewish monotheism. They also saw little evidence that the Age to Come had arrived. Gradually, Jewish and Christian communities became distinct.

- Over the centuries, and for many complex reasons, the relationship between the Jewish and Christian peoples has been a scandalous example to the world of oppression and victimization. Christians taught that God had cursed Jews. Jews were marginalized in Christian society and suffered periodic persecution.

- After the Nazi genocide against Jews in the twentieth century, Christian communities began a major reform of their understanding and teachings of Judaism.

- Most came to realize that the people of Israel remain in covenant with a God who is eternally faithful. Both Jews and Christians live covenanting lives with God. In various ways, they follow the traditions of rabbis in fulfilling their covenanting duties and mission in their world. They both celebrate their covenanting life with God in worship and liturgy. God summons and empowers both Jews and Christians to oppose the sinful aspects of human societies, including those within their own communities.

- Jews and Christians are required by God to be in right relationship with each other in order to undertake their mission to be light to the nations and to prepare the world for its salvific destiny—the life of the Age to Come. By dwelling in shalom, they will be doing God's will by helping to prepare for universal shalom.

# Notes

1. Mary C. Boys has also developed a synthesis of what she calls the "conventional account" of Christian origins. Although containing different elements than my own, she, too, has concluded that it is supersessionist. See her *Jewish-Christian Dialogue: One Woman's Experience—The 1997 Madeleva Lecture in Spirituality* (New York/Mahwah, N.J.: Paulist Press, 1997), pp. 81–85. Similarly, R. Kendall Soulen has noted that the overarching Christian master reading of the Bible has been "a drama in four acts: creation, fall, redemption in Christ Jesus, and final consummation." He likewise deems this construal to be supersessionist. See his "Removing Anti-Judaism" in Howard Clark Kee and Irvin J. Borowsky, eds., *Removing Anti-Judaism from the New Testament* (Philadelphia: American Interfaith Institute/World Alliance, 1998), p. 151.

2. For more on this social situation, see these works by Robert L. Wilken, *The Christians as the Romans Saw Them* (New Haven: Yale University Press, 1984); *John Chrysostom and the Jews: Rhetoric and Reality in the Fourth Century* (Berkeley: University of California Press, 1983); and *Judaism and the Early Christian Mind: A Study of Cyril of Alexandria's Exegesis and Theology* (New Haven: Yale University Press, 1971). See also David P. Efroymson, "The Patristic Connection," in Alan T. Davies, ed., *AntiSemitism and the Foundations of Christianity* (New York/Ramsey/Toronto: Paulist Press, 1979), pp. 98–117 and his forthcoming work on patristic homilies and commentaries that were not explicitly styled as *"adversus Judaeos"* materials.

3. This volume will employ the terms *Shared Testament* and *Christian Testament* for the scriptural collections usually known as the "Old" and "New" Testaments. See the introduction in my *The Hebrew*

*Scriptures and the Lectionary: Interpreting the "Old Testament" as a "Shared Testament"* (New York/Mahwah, N.J.: Paulist Press, forthcoming) for a detailed explanation.

4. Pier Francesco Fumagalli, *"Nostra Aetate:* A Milestone,"* delivered at the Vatican Symposium on *The Roots of Anti-Judaism in the Christian Environment,* October 31, 1997.

5. Origen, *Contra Celsum,* IV, 22.

6. NCCB, "Statement" (1975), Nos. 2, 8.

7. Edward Cardinal Idris Cassidy, "Reflections: The Vatican Statement on the Shoah," in *Origins* 28/2 (May 28, 1998): 31.

8. For collections of ecclesial documents from a large number of Christian denominations, see Helga Croner, ed., *Stepping Stones to Further Jewish-Christian Relations: An Unabridged Collection of Christian Documents* and *More Stepping Stones to Jewish-Christian Relations: An Unabridged Collection of Christian Documents 1975–1983* (New York/Mahwah, N.J.: Paulist Press/Stimulus Books, 1977 and 1985); World Council of Churches, *The Theology of the Churches and the Jewish People* (Geneva: WCC Publications, 1988).

9. "Address to the Jewish Community—West Germany" (Nov. 17, 1980), p. 15.

10. Ibid.

11. Idem, "Address to Jewish Leaders in Miami" (Sept. 11, 1987), p. 105.

12. E.g., "[Christians must] strive to learn by what essential traits the Jews *define themselves in the light of their own religious experience"* (Vatican, "Guidelines" [1974], Preamble, emphasis added); "There is special urgency for Christians to listen...to ways in which Jews understand their history and their traditions, their faith and their obedience 'in their own terms'" (WCC, "Ecumenical Considerations" [1982], 1.7); "I think that in this sense you [the Jewish people] continue your particular vocation, showing yourselves to be still the heirs of that election to which God is faithful. This is your mission in the contemporary world before the peoples, the nations, all of humanity, the church" (John Paul II, "Address to Jewish Leaders in Warsaw" [June 14, 1987], p. 99).

13. [West] German Bishops' Conference, "The Church and the Jews" (1980), I.

14. WCC, "The Church and the Jewish People" (1967), V.

15. Ibid., III.

16. PBC, "Interpretation" (1993), I,A, II,B,1.

17. See note 3.

18. NCCB, *God's Mercy* (1988), 31c. Note also, "Typological reading only manifests the unfathomable riches of the Old Testament, its inexhaustible content and the mystery of which it is full, and should not lead us to forget that it retains its own value as revelation that the New Testament often does no more than resume" (Vatican, "Notes" [1985], II,7).

19. *New St. Joseph Edition of the Baltimore Catechism,* No. 2 (New York: Catholic Book Publishing, 1962), pp. 36, 46.

20. Richard J. Clifford and Roland E. Murphy, "Genesis," in Raymond E. Brown, Joseph A. Fitzmyer, and Roland E. Murphy, eds., *The New Jerome Biblical Commentary* (Englewood Cliffs, N.J.: Prentice Hall, 1990), p. 12. This volume is a compendium of centrist biblical scholarship. As further examples, see also Walter Brueggemann, *Genesis,* Interpretation Bible Commentary (Atlanta: John Knox Press, 1982), p. 46; Robert B. Coote and David Robert Ord, *The Bible's First History* (Philadelphia: Fortress Press, 1989), p. 63; and E. A. Speiser, *Genesis,* Anchor Bible Commentary (New York: Doubleday, 1964), p. 24.

21. PBC, "Interpretation" (1993), II,B,1.

22. See David P. Efroymson, Eugene J. Fisher, and Leon Klenicki, eds., *Within Context: Essays on Jews and Judaism in the New Testament* (Philadelphia: American Interfaith Institute, 1993).

23. PBC, "Interpretation" (1993), IV,A,3. It seems logically inescapable that this principle must also relate to the texts of the Shared Testament. So to apply it to the example of Genesis 3:15, a construal of that passage in an exclusively christological fashion would not only maintain a now-rejected supersessionist version of the Christian story, it would also disrespect the inherent revelatory value of the inspired texts of ancient Israel on their own terms. Unfavorable attitudes to Judaism would thereby be promoted.

24. Joseph Stephen O'Leary, *Questioning Back: The Overcoming of Metaphysics in Christian Tradition* (Minneapolis/Chicago/New York: Winston Press, 1985), p. 73.

25. Note, for example: "Timebound humanity must recognize that no interpretation from one time, place, and language is ever translatable without remainder into another time, place, and language....We can never escape our particularity in our interpretation. However, today as we try to respond to the rise of historical consciousness, we bear the burden of

many centuries in which faith has sought understanding in the categories of timeless metaphysics." Bernard J. Lee, *Jesus and the Metaphors of God: The Christs of the New Testament,* Volume 2, *Conversation on the Road Not Taken* (New York/Mahwah, N.J.: Paulist Press/ Stimulus Books, 1993), p. 19.

26. O'Leary, *Questioning Back,* p. 76.

27. See Vatican Council II, Gaudium et Spes, 4, "In language *intelligible to every generation,* [the church] should be able to answer the ever recurring questions which people ask about the meaning of this present life and of the life to come, and how one is related to the other." Emphasis added.

28. John Paul II, *Fides et Ratio,* 12 in Origins 28/19 (October 22, 1998): 321–22.

29. Note this comment in PBC, "Interpretation" (1993), III,B,2, "The allegorical interpretation of Scripture so characteristic of patristic exegesis runs the risk of being something of an embarrassment to people today. But the experience of the church expressed in this exegesis makes a contribution that is always useful...."

30. Bernard J. Lee, *The Galilean Jewishness of Jesus: Retrieving the Jewish Origins of Christianity,* Volume 1, *Conversation on the Road Not Taken* (New York/Mahwah, N.J.: Paulist Press/Stimulus Books, 1988), p. 25.

31. NCCB, "Statement" (1975). An illustration of "de-Judaizing" may be seen in the Nicene Creed. It asserted both the humanity and divinity of Christ using ontological terminology, but never mentions Israel or that Jesus was a Jew.

32. O'Leary, *Questioning Back,* pp. 128–29.

33. Note the words of John Paul II, who in discussing the incarnational nature of divine revelations observes, "[O]ur vision of the face of God is always fragmentary and impaired by the limits of our understanding. Faith alone makes it possible to penetrate the mystery in a way that allows us to understand it coherently" (*Fides et Ratio,* 13). Biblically, faith is being in relationship with God because of the grace that God extends to enter into such a relationship. It is relationship with God that allows a congruent understanding of God's revelatory self-disclosures.

34. See Paul M. van Buren, *Christ in Context,* Volume 3, *A Theology of the Jewish-Christian Reality* (San Francisco: Harper & Row, 1988), pp. 257–58, who in a discussion of the unity between the

Father and the Son observes: "If it is predetermined that reality is to be analyzed in terms of *hypostasis* (substance or subsistence) and *physis* (nature), then the hypostatic union will be judged ontological and the unity of the covenant [or relationship] only volitional. If, on the other hand, reality is analyzed in personal terms with the relationship of love between human beings taken as the highest visible form, if reality consists primarily of relationships of love and trust and forgiveness, and then, only secondarily, of material relationships, then it could be said that the covenantal model of unity is indeed ontological by its own metaphysical presuppositions." Note also John Paul II in *Fides et Ratio,* 32: "[B]elief is often humanly richer than mere evidence because it involves *an interpersonal relationship* and brings into play not only a person's capacity to know, but also the deeper capacity to entrust oneself to others, to enter into a relationship with them which is intimate and enduring." Emphasis added.

35. This term is used in Catherine Mowry LaCugna, *God for Us: The Trinity and Christian Life* (New York: HarperCollins, 1991). E.g., "A relational ontology establishes that no person can be thought of by himself or herself, apart from other persons. Even less can we reify the person of the Spirit, trying to point out what the Spirit is in and by himself or herself....God's immutability is God's fidelity, both to be God and to be God-for-us. God remains eternally faithful to the Covenant made with Israel. God's self-given name, YHWH, speaks of God's promise always to be with Israel. For Christians, Jesus Christ is the definitive and fully personal sign of God's everlasting fidelity to-be-with-us. The Spirit is divine fidelity in action, as the Spirit leads all creatures into an ever-deeper communion with each other and with God" (pp. 298, 301–2).

36. John Paul II, "Evolution" (1996), 4. The only provisos put on a Catholic's acceptance of evolution are that the existence of God or of the divinely created individual human soul not be denied.

37. John Haught, "Evolution's Impact on Theology," in *Origins* 27/34 (February 12, 1998): 576.

38. E.g., Nahum M. Sarna, *Genesis,* The JPS Torah Commentary (Philadelphia/New York/Jerusalem: Jewish Publication Society, 1989), p. 15, notes rabbinic commentators who understood Genesis 2:2 to mean that humans must now continue God's creative activity. Similarly, Irving Greenberg, *The Jewish Way: Living the Holidays* (New York: Summit Books, 1988), p. 95, observes: "God places the future of creation into our

hands now because humans have infinite value now, and not just when humanity is perfected. The processes of *tikkun olam* (perfecting the world) and *tikkun ha-adam* (perfecting humanity) go on side by side and reinforce each other."

39. E.g., see Coote and Ord, *The Bible's First History,* pp. 42–64.

40. In this regard note the comments of John Paul II, "Galileo" (1992), 8, "It is a duty for theologians to keep themselves regularly informed of scientific advances in order to examine, if such be necessary, whether or not there are reasons for taking them into account in their reflection or for introducing changes in their teaching." See also Vatican Council II, *Gaudium et Spes* (1965), 5, "Humankind substitutes a dynamic and more evolutionary concept of nature for a static one, and the result is an immense series of new problems calling for a new endeavor of analysis and synthesis."

41. *CCC* (1994), par. 390—italics in the original, cf. GS1351.

42. Ibid., par. 1008.

43. See my *Education for Shalom: Religion Textbooks and the Enhancement of the Catholic and Jewish Relationship* (Collegeville, Minn.: Liturgical Press, 1995).

44. Here is a recent example of this teaching: "No one can remain indifferent [to the *Shoah*], least of all the Church, by reason of her *very close bonds* of spiritual kinship with the Jewish people and her remembrance of the injustices of the past. The Church's relationship to the Jewish people is unlike the one she shares with any other religions....Looking to the future of relations between Christians and Jews, in the first place we appeal to our Catholic brothers and sisters to renew the awareness of *the Hebrew roots of their faith.* We ask them to keep in mind that Jesus was a descendant of David; that the Virgin Mary and the Apostles belonged to the Jewish people; that the Church draws sustenance from the root of that good olive tree on to which have been grafted the wild olive branches of the Gentiles (cf. Romans 11:17–24); that *the Jews are our dearly beloved brothers, indeed in a certain sense they are 'our elder brothers' "* (Vatican, *We Remember* [1998], I,V, emphasis added).

45. John Paul II, *Tertio Millennio Adveniente,* 33.

46. The others are *Education for Shalom; Proclaiming Shalom: Lectionary Introductions to Foster the Catholic and Jewish Relationship* (Collegeville, Minn., Liturgical Press, 1995); and *Sharing Shalom: A Process for Local Interfaith Dialogue Between Christians*

*and Jews,* edited with Rabbi Arthur F. Starr (New York/Mahwah, N.J.: Paulist Press/Stimulus Books, 1998).

47.  Edward Cardinal Idris Cassidy, "Reflections: The Vatican Statement on the Shoah," in *Origins* 28/2 (May 28, 1998): 31.

48.  John Paul II, "Prayer at the Western Wall," March 26, 2000.

49.  Vatican Council II, *Gaudium et Spes,* 12: "For sacred scripture teaches that women and men were created 'in the image of God,' able to know and love their creator, and set by him over all earthly creatures that they might rule over them, and make use of them, while glorifying God."

50.  Ibid., "For by their innermost nature men and women are social beings; and if they do not enter into relationships with others they can neither live nor develop their gifts."

51.  Ibid., 17, "[G]enuine Freedom is an exceptional sign of the image of God in humanity. For God willed that men and women should be left free to make their own decisions so that they might attain their full and blessed perfection by cleaving to God. Their dignity requires them to act out of conscious and free choice...."

52.  Ibid., 13, "[W]hen people look into their own hearts they find that they are drawn towards what is wrong and are sunk in many evils which cannot have come from their good creator. Often refusing to acknowledge God as their source, men and women have also upset the relationship which should link them to their final destiny; and at the same time they have broken the right order that should exist within themselves as well as between them and other people and all creatures. They are therefore divided interiorly. As a result, the entire life of women and men, both individual and social, shows itself to be a struggle, and a dramatic one, between good and evil, between light and darkness."

53.  NCCB, *Economic Justice* (1986), 33, "The Bible castigates not only the worship of idols, but also manifestations of idolatry, such as the quest for unrestrained power and the desire for great wealth (Isa 40:12–20; 44:1–20; Wis 13:1–14:31; Col 3:5, 'the greed that is idolatry')....Alienation from God pits brother against brother (Gen 4:8–16), in a cycle of war and vengeance (Gen 4:22–23)....Sin simultaneously alienates human beings from God and shatters the solidarity of the human community."

54.  John Paul II, *Fides et Ratio,* 22, "[T]he apostle [Paul] declares a profound truth: Through all that is created, the 'eyes of the mind' can

come to know God. Through the medium of creatures, God stirs in reason an intuition of his 'power' and his 'divinity' (cf. Rom. 1:20)."

55. Ibid.13, "By the authority of his absolute transcendence, God who makes himself known is also the source of the credibility of what he reveals. By faith, men and women give their assent to this divine testimony. This means that they acknowledge fully and integrally the truth of what is revealed because it is God himself who is the guarantor of that truth. They can make no claim upon this truth, which comes to them as a gift and which, set within the context of interpersonal communication, urges reason to be open to it and embrace its profound meaning."

56. This last sentence is indebted to Michael Wyschogrod, *The Body of Faith: Judaism as Corporeal Election* (Minneapolis: Winston Press, 1983), pp. 212, 213–14: "God dwells in Israel.... He envelops Israel. Israel is Hashem's abode in the created world....Hashem's indwelling in Israel is not the incarnation of Christianity, which results in a sinless Christ. Hashem's indwelling in Israel is 'in the midst of their uncleanness.' The sin of Israel is not dissipated by the divine indwelling. It is, in fact, heightened. To be the people through whom Hashem acts in history and yet not to be perfectly obedient, indeed to be very disobedient, is a terrible fact....But it is not a fact that drives the divine indwelling out. Hashem continues to dwell in and with this people...."

57. NCCB, *Economic Justice* (1986), 38, "Central to the biblical presentation of justice is that the justice of a community is measured by its treatment of the powerless in society, most often described as the widow, the orphan, the poor, and the stranger (non-Israelite) in the land. The Law, the Prophets, and the Wisdom literature…all show deep concern for the proper treatment of such people."

58. Ibid., 36, "The codes of Israel reflect the norms of the covenant: reciprocal responsibility, mercy, and truthfulness. They embody a life in freedom from oppression: worship of the One God, rejection of idolatry, mutual respect among people, care and protection for every member of the social body. Being free and being a co-responsible community are God's intentions for us."

59. Wyschogrod, *Body of Faith,* 175, "God is the Lord of Israel while Israel is the servant of God. Nevertheless, God appears in history as the God of Israel and there can therefore be no thought about God that is not also thought about Israel."

60. NCCB, *Economic Justice* (1986), 37, "When the people turn away from the living God to serve idols and no longer heed the commands of the covenant, God sends prophets to recall his saving deeds and to summon them to return to the one who betrothed them 'in right and in justice, in love and in mercy' (Hos 2:21). The substance of prophetic faith is proclaimed by Micah: 'to do justice and to love kindness, and to walk humbly with your God' (Mi 6:8, RSV). Biblical faith in general, and prophetic faith especially, insist that fidelity to the covenant joins obedience to God with reverence and concern for the neighbor."

61. PBC, "Bible and Christology" (1984), 2,1,2,2, "Though David's successors scarcely followed in his footsteps, the prophets looked forward to that king who, as David had done (2 Sam 8:15), would administer equity and justice, especially to the poorest and the lowliest of the realm (Isa 9:5–6; Jer 23:5–6; 33:15–16)."

62. PBC, "Interpretation" (1993), I,A,1, "Literary criticism for a long time came to be identified with the attempt to distinguish in texts different sources. Thus it was that there developed in the 19th century the 'documentary hypothesis,' which sought to give an explanation of the editing of the Pentateuch. According to this hypothesis, four documents, to some extent parallel with each other, had been woven together: that of the Yahwist (J), that of the Elohist (E), that of the Deuteronomist (D) and that of the priestly author (P); the final editor made use of this final (priestly) document to provide a structure for the whole....In [its] essential features, [the hypothesis] retain[s]...prominence in scientific exegesis today—though...under challenge."

63. Vatican, "Notes," 12, "Jesus was and always remained a Jew, his ministry was deliberately limited 'to the lost sheep of the house of Israel' (Mt 15:24). Jesus is fully a man of his time and of his environment—the Jewish Palestinian one of the first century, the anxieties and hopes of which he shared." In referring to the Shared Testament, Pope John Paul II has observed that Jesus "came humanly to know these texts; he nourished his mind and heart with them, using them in prayer and as an inspiration for his actions" ("PBC Address" [1997]). See also PBC, "Bible and Christology" (1984), 1,2,5, "The diligent study of Judaism is of utmost importance for the correct understanding of the person of Jesus, as well as of the early Church and its specific faith."

64. PBC, "Bible and Christology" (1984), 2,2,2, "The faith of Jesus' disciples...was completely shattered at his death, as all the

Gospels testify. Yet it emerged more fully and clearly once God raised him from the dead and granted him to be seen by his disciples (Acts 10:40 ff; cf. 1.3; Jn 20:19–29). The appearances, in which Jesus "presented himself alive with many proofs after his passion" (Acts 1:3), were in no way expected by the disciples, with the result that 'they accepted the truth of his resurrection only with hesitation' (Leo the Great, Serm. 61:4; cf. Mt 28:17; Lk 24:11)."

65. NCCB et al., *Within Context* (1987), "[T]he New Testament authors sought to explain their experience of Jesus in terms of their Jewish heritage, especially by using passages from the Hebrew Scriptures....Such post-Resurrection insights do not replace the original intentions of the prophets."

66. PBC, "Bible and Christology" (1984), 1,2,6,2, "This ["decision of faith"] must be applied in a special way to the resurrection of Christ, which cannot be proved in an empirical way. For by it Jesus is introduced into 'the world to come.'"

67. PBC, "Gospels" (1964), 9, "From many things handed down [the Gospel writers] selected some things, reduced others to a synthesis, others they explicated as they kept in mind the situation of the churches....Indeed, from what they had received the sacred writers above all selected the things which were suited to the various situations of the faithful and to the purpose which they had in mind, and adapted their narration of them to the same situations and purpose."

68. Vatican, "Notes," 21, "The Gospels are the outcome of long and complicated editorial work....Hence it cannot be ruled out that some references hostile to the Jews have their historical context in conflicts between the nascent church and the Jewish community. Certain controversies reflect Christian-Jewish relations long after the time of Jesus. To establish this is of capital importance if we wish to bring out the meaning of certain Gospel texts for Christians today."

69. For this paragraph I am indebted to Irving J. Greenberg, "The Relationship of Judaism and Christianity: Toward a New Organic Model," in Eugene J. Fisher, A. James Rudin, and Marc H. Tanenbaum, eds., *Twenty Years of Jewish-Catholic Relations* (New York/Mahwah, N.J.: Paulist Press, 1986): pp. 191–211.

70. Vatican, *We Remember* (1998), III, "Christian mobs who attacked pagan temples sometimes did the same to synagogues, not without being influenced by certain interpretations of the New Testament

regarding the Jewish people as a whole. 'In the Christian world...erroneous and unjust interpretations of the New Testament regarding the Jewish people and their alleged culpability have circulated for too long, engendering feelings of hostility towards this people' [John Paul II, "Speech to Symposium on the Roots of Anti-Judaism in the Christian Milieu," October 21, 1997]. Such interpretations of the New Testament have been totally and definitively rejected by the Second Vatican Council."

71. The Catholic Church, and most other denominations, of course reject this contention today. See, e.g., Vatican, "Notes" (1985), I,3, "The Holy Father has stated this permanent reality of the Jewish people in a remarkable theological formula, in his allocution to the Jewish community of West Germany at Mainz, on November 17, 1980: '...the people of God of the Old Covenant, which has never been revoked....'"

72. Vatican Council II, *Unitatis Redintegratio,* 14, "[T]he heritage handed down by the apostles was received differently and in different forms, so that from the very beginnings of the church its development varied from region to region and also because of differing mentalities and ways of life. These reasons, plus external causes, as well as the lack of charity and mutual understanding, left the way open to divisions."

73. Vatican, *We Remember* (1998), III, "Despite the Christian preaching of love for all, even for one's enemies, the prevailing mentality down the centuries penalized minorities and those who were in any way 'different.' Sentiments of anti-Judaism in some Christian quarters, and the gap which existed between the Church and the Jewish people, led to a generalized discrimination, which ended at times in expulsions or attempts at forced conversions. In a large part of the 'Christian' world, until the end of the 18th century, those who were not Christian did not always enjoy a fully guaranteed juridical status. Despite that fact, the Jews throughout Christendom held on to their religious traditions and communal customs. They were therefore looked upon with a certain suspicion and mistrust. In times of crisis such as famine, war, pestilence or social tensions, the Jewish minority was sometimes taken as a scapegoat and became the victim of violence, looting, and even massacres."

74. John Paul II, "Galileo" (1992), 6,12, "The birth of a new way of approaching the study of natural phenomena demands a clarification on the part of all disciplines of knowledge. It obliges them to define more clearly their own field, their approach, their methods, as well as the import of their conclusions. In other words, this new way requires

each discipline to become more rigorously aware of its own nature....The error of the theologians of the time when they maintained the centrality of the Earth was to think that our understanding of the physical world's structure was in some way imposed by the literal sense of Sacred Scripture."

75. Vatican, "Ecumenism" (1993), 18, "Human folly and human sinfulness...have at times opposed the unifying purpose of the Holy Spirit and weakened that power of love which overcomes the inherent tensions in ecclesial life. From the beginning of the church, certain rifts came into being....The Decree on Ecumenism recognizes that some dissensions have come about 'for which often enough people on both sides were to blame.' Yet, however much human culpability has damaged communion, it has never destroyed it."

76. John Paul II, "Evolution" (1996), "[N]ew knowledge leads to the recognition of the theory of evolution as more than a hypothesis. It is indeed remarkable that this theory has been progressively accepted by researchers following a series of discoveries in various fields of knowledge. The convergence, neither sought nor provoked, of the results of work that was conducted independently is itself a significant argument in favor of this theory." Note: Vatican Council II, *Gaudium et Spes* (1965), 5, "Humankind substitutes a dynamic and more evolutionary concept of nature for a static one, and the result is an immense series of new problems calling for a new endeavor of analysis and synthesis."

77. Vatican, *We Remember* (1998), II, "While bearing unique witness to the Holy One of Israel and to the Torah, the Jewish people have suffered much at different times and in many places. But the Shoah was certainly the worst suffering of all. The inhumanity with which the Jews were persecuted and massacred during this century is beyond the capacity of words to convey. All this was done to them for the sole reason that they were Jews."

78. Ibid., 2, "The very magnitude of the [Shoah] raises many questions....Much scholarly study remains to be done. But such an event cannot be fully measured by the ordinary criteria of historical research alone. It calls for a 'moral and religious memory' and, particularly among Christians, a very serious reflection on what gave rise to it. The fact that the Shoah took place in Europe, that is, in countries of long-standing Christian civilization, raises the question of the relation

between the Nazi persecution and the attitudes down the centuries of Christians towards Jews."

79. Vatican Council II, *Nostra Aetate,* 4.

80. E.g., Michael McGarry, "Roman Catholic Understandings of Mission," in Martin A. Cohen and Helga Croner, eds., *Christian Mission—Jewish Mission* (New York/Ramsey, N.J.: Paulist Press/Stimulus Books, 1982), p. 142.

81. E.g., Paul M. van Buren, *A Christian Theology of the People Israel, Volume 2, A Theology of the Jewish-Christian Reality* (New York: Seabury Press, 1983), pp. 350–52.

82. E.g., Greenberg, "The Relationship of Judaism and Christianity," p. 207 ff.

83. See Leon Klenicki, "On Christianity—Toward a Process of Spiritual and Historical Healing: Understanding the Other as a Person of God," *In Dialogue,* 1992, No. 1: 19–36.

84. John Paul II, "Address to the Jewish Community—West Germany," (1980), p. 16, "Jews and Christians, as children of Abraham, are called to be a blessing for the world [cf. Gen. 12:2 ff.], by committing themselves together for peace and justice among all men and peoples, with the fullness and depth that God intended us to have, and with readiness for sacrifices that this goal may demand."

85. John Paul II, "Prayer at the Western Wall," March 26, 2000.

86. Note these comments of John Paul II to the 16th meeting of the International Catholic-Jewish Liaison Committee in Vatican City, March 26, 1998: "The progress you have already made shows the immense promise held out by continuing dialogue between Jews and Catholics. But your work is also an impressive sign of hope to a world marked by conflict and division....A commitment to authentic dialogue, rooted in a sincere love of truth and an openness to all the members of the human family, remains the first and indispensable path to the reconciliation and peace that the world needs."

87. Greenberg, "The Relationship of Judaism and Christianity," pp. 207–11.

88. Note these pertinent comments of Pope John Paul II, "By the authority of his absolute transcendence, God who makes himself known is also the source of the credibility of what he reveals. By faith, men and women give their assent to this divine testimony. This means that they acknowledge fully and integrally the truth of what is revealed because it

is God himself who is the guarantor of that truth. They can make no claim upon this truth, which comes to them as a gift and which, set within the context of interpersonal communication, urges reason to be open to it and embrace its profound meaning" (*Fides et Ratio,* 13).

89. PBC, "Bible and Christology," 1,2,6,2, "This ["decision of faith"] must be applied in a special way to the resurrection of Christ, which by its very nature cannot be proved in an empirical way....[O]ne may not simplify this question excessively, as if any historian, making use only of scientific investigation, could prove it with certainty as a fact accessible to any observer whatsoever. In this matter there is also needed 'the decision of faith' or better 'an open heart,' so that the mind may be moved to assent."

90. For more on the subtlety of divine self-disclosure, see Samuel Therrien, *The Elusive Presence: Toward a New Biblical Theology* (New York/Hagerstown, Md./San Francisco/London: Harper & Row, 1978). For an interreligious, philosophical-theological approach to the human knowing of God, see David B. Burrell, *Knowing the Unknowable God: Ibn-Sina, Maimonides, Aquinas* (Notre Dame, Ind.: University of Notre Dame Press, 1986).

91. See Raymond E. Brown, *The Virginal Conception and Bodily Resurrection of Jesus* (New York: Paulist Press, 1973), pp. 69–129; and Pheme Perkins, *Resurrection: New Testament Witness and Contemporary Reflection* (Garden City, N.Y.: Doubleday, 1984), esp. pp. 71–330.

92. Note these comments of the Pontifical Biblical Commission, "Sacred Scripture is in dialogue with communities of believers: It has come from their traditions of faith....Dialogue with Scripture in its entirety, which means dialogue with the understanding of the faith prevailing in earlier times, must be matched by a dialogue with the generation of today. Such dialogue will mean establishing a relationship of continuity. It will also involve acknowledging differences. Hence the interpretation of Scripture involves a work of sifting and setting aside; it stands in continuity with earlier exegetical traditions, many elements of which it preserves and makes its own; but in other matters it will go its own way, seeking to make further progress" (PBC, "Interpretation," III,A,3).

93. For this section I am profoundly indebted to Sandra M. Schneiders, *The Revelatory Text: Interpreting the New Testament as Sacred Scripture* (San Francisco: HarperSanFrancisco, 1991).

94. PBC, "Interpretation," III,A,1.

95. Ibid.

96. John Paul II, *Fides et Ratio,* 49.

97. NCCB, *God's Mercy* (1988), 8: "[F]alse or demeaning portraits of a repudiated Israel may undermine Christianity as well. How can one confidently affirm the truth of God's covenant with all humanity and creation in Christ (see Rom 8:21) without at the same time affirming God's faithfulness to the Covenant with Israel that also lies at the heart of the biblical testimony?"

98. John Paul II, "Address to Jewish Leaders in Miami" (Sept. 11, 1987), p. 105.

99. See N. T. Wright, "Adam, Israel, and the Messiah," *The Climax of the Covenant* (Minneapolis: Fortress Press, 1993), pp. 18–40.

100. [West] German Bishops' Conference, "The Church and the Jews" (1980), I.

101. John Paul II, "PBC Address" (1997).

102. NCCB, *God's Mercy* (1988), 31c. Note also, "Typological reading only manifests the unfathomable riches of the Old Testament, its inexhaustible content and the mystery of which it is full, and should not lead us to forget that it retains its own value as revelation that the New Testament often does not more than resume" (Vatican, "Notes" [1985], II,7).

103. Vatican, "Notes" (1985), II,7.

104. Vatican, "Guidelines" (1974), Preamble.

105. CDF, *Dominus Iesus* (2000), II,10, citing John Paul II, *Redemptoris Missio,* 55.

106. Ibid.

107. Ibid.

108. Perhaps most powerfully articulated by John Paul II, "Address at the Great Synagogue of Rome" (April 13, 1986), 4: "...the Church of Christ discovers her 'bond' with Judaism by 'searching into her own mystery' (cf. *Nostra Aetate,* ibid.) The Jewish religion is not 'extrinsic' to us, but in a certain way is 'intrinsic' to our own religion. With Judaism therefore we have a relationship which we do not have with any other religion. You are our dearly beloved brothers and, in a certain way, it could be said that you are our elder brothers."

109. A related question on the relationship of Jesus Christ to the world religions other than Judaism and Christianity is beyond the parameters of this book. See CDF, *Dominus Iesus* (2000) for the most

recent magisterial statement on that subject, which, very interestingly, did not seem to classify Judaism as "non-Christian" because of its deep spiritual bonds with the church.

110. Vatican,"Notes" (1985), II,9.

111. Ibid., II,8.

112. Ibid., II,10–11.

113. See the helpful summary in John Pawlikowski, *Jesus and the Theology of Israel* (Wilmington, Del.: Michael Glazier, 1989), pp. 15–47. Note: Vatican "Notes" (1986), I,7: "Church and Judaism cannot be seen as two parallel ways of salvation...."

114. Vatican "Guidelines" (1974), Preamble.

115. Peter von der Osten-Sacken, *Christian-Jewish Dialogue,* Margaret Kohl, trans. (Philadelphia: Fortress Press, 1986), pp. 80–81. Italics in the original.

116. Even in the relatively brief time since Christians began renouncing supersessionism, some Jewish scholars have begun to grapple with this subject. E.g., "We [Jews] are no longer alone in performing our central task of religious witness. Christians stand today by our side as upbuilders of the Kingdom. They have spread the knowledge of Israel's God across the Western world and beyond. How did this happen? What does it mean for the world and for us?" (Michael S. Kogan, "Toward a Jewish Theology of Christianity," *Journal of Ecumenical Studies* 32/1 [Winter 1995]: 95).

117. "I think that in this sense you [the Jewish people] continue your particular vocation, showing yourselves to be still the heirs of that election to which God is faithful. This is your mission in the contemporary world before the peoples, the nations, all of humanity, the church" (John Paul II, "Address to Jewish Leaders in Warsaw" [June 14, 1987], p. 99).

118. "The permanence of Israel (while so many ancient peoples have disappeared without trace) is a historic fact and a sign to be interpreted within God's design." Vatican "Notes" (1985), VI,25.

119. For detailed recommendations for Christians about teaching and preaching on Jews and Judaism, see my *Education for Shalom* (Collegeville, Minn.: Liturgical Press, 1995), pp. 121–35.

# Works Consulted

Bausch, William J. *Pilgrim Church: A Popular History of Catholic Christianity.* Rev. and exp. ed. Mystic, Conn.: Twenty-Third Publications, 1994.

Bernier, Paul. *Ministry in the Church: A Historical and Pastoral Approach.* Mystic, Conn.: Twenty-Third Publications, 1992.

Blenkinsopp, Joseph. *A History of Prophecy in Israel: From the Settlement in the Land to the Hellenistic Period.* Philadelphia: Westminster Press, 1983.

Borowitz, Eugene B. *Renewing the Covenant: A Theology for the Postmodern Jew.* Philadelphia/New York/Jerusalem: Jewish Publication Society, 1991.

Boys, Mary C. *Jewish-Christian Dialogue: One Woman's Experience—The 1997 Madeleva Lecture in Spirituality.* New York/Mahwah, N.J.: Paulist Press, 1997.

Brown, Raymond E. *The Virginal Conception and Bodily Resurrection of Jesus.* New York: Paulist Press, 1973.

Brueggemann, Walter. *Genesis.* Interpretation Bible Commentary. Atlanta: John Knox Press, 1982.

Burrell, David B. *Knowing the Unknowable God: Ibn-Sina, Maimonides, Aquinas.* Notre Dame, Ind.: University of Notre Dame Press, 1986.

Cartmill, Matt. "The Gift of Gab." *Discovery.* November 1998: 56–64.

Cassidy, Edward Cardinal Idris. "Reflections: The Vatican Statement on the *Shoah.*" *Origins* 28/2 (May 28, 1998): 28–32.

Clifford, Richard J., and Roland E. Murphy. "Genesis." Raymond E. Brown, Joseph A. Fitzmyer, and Roland E. Murphy, eds. *The New Jerome Biblical Commentary.* Englewood Cliffs, N.J.: Prentice Hall, 1990: pp. 8–43.

Coote, Robert B. *Early Israel: A New Horizon.* Minneapolis: Fortress Press, 1990.

Coote, Robert B., and Mary P. Coote. *Power, Politics, and the Making of the Bible: An Introduction.* Minneapolis: Fortress Press, 1990.

Coote, Robert B., and David Robert Ord. *The Bible's First History: From Creation to the Court of David with the Yahwist.* Philadelphia: Fortress Press, 1989.

Efroymson, David P. "The Patristic Connection" in Alan T. Davies, ed., *AntiSemitism and the Foundations of Christianity.* New York/Ramsey, N.J./Toronto: Paulist Press, 1979.

Efroymson, David P., Eugene J. Fisher, and Leon Klenicki, eds. *Within Context: Essays on Jews and Judaism in the New Testament.* Philadelphia: American Interfaith Institute, 1993.

Flannery, Edward H. *The Anguish of the Jews: Twenty-Three Centuries of Antisemitism.* Rev. and updated. New York/Mahwah, N.J.: Paulist Press/Stimulus, 1985.

Freedman, David H. "The Mysterious Middle of the Milky Way." *Discover.* November 1998: 66–75.

Fumagalli, Pier Francesco. "*Nostra Aetate*: A Milestone." Delivered at the Vatican Symposium on *The Roots of Anti-Judaism in the Christian Environment.* October 31, 1997. http://www.vatican.va/jubilee_2000/magazine/ju_mag_01111997_p-31_it.shtml

Gottwald, Norman. *The Hebrew Bible: A Socio-Literary Introduction.* Philadelphia: Fortress Press, 1985.

Greenberg, Irving. *The Jewish Way: Living the Holidays.* New York: Summit Books, 1988.

———. "The Relationship of Judaism and Christianity: Toward a New Organic Model." Eugene J. Fisher, A. James Rudin, and Marc H. Tanenbaum, eds., *Twenty Years of Jewish-Catholic Relations.* New York/Mahwah, N.J.: Paulist Press, 1986: 191–211.

Haught, John. "Evolution's Impact on Theology." *Origins* 27/34 (February 12, 1998): 574–77.

Hawking, Stephen W. *A Brief History of Time: From the Big Bang to Black Holes.* New York: Bantam Books, 1988.

Horsley, Richard A. *Jesus and the Spiral of Violence: Popular Jewish Resistance in Roman Palestine.* San Francisco: Harper & Row, 1987.

Horsley, Richard A., with John S. Hanson. *Bandits, Prophets, and Messiahs: Popular Movements at the Time of Jesus.* San Francisco: Harper & Row, 1985.

Hurtado, Larry W. *One God, One Lord: Early Christian Devotion and Ancient Jewish Monotheism.* Philadelphia: Fortress Press, 1988.

Johanson, Donald, and Maitland Edey. *Lucy: The Beginnings of Humankind.* New York: Simon and Schuster, 1981.

Klenicki, Leon. "On Christianity—Toward a Process of Spiritual and Historical Healing: Understanding the Other as a Person of God." *In Dialogue,* 1992, No. 1: 19–36.

Kogan, Michael S. "Toward a Jewish Theology of Christianity." *Journal of Ecumenical Studies* 32/1 (Winter 1995): 89–106.

LaCugna, Catherine Mowry. *God for Us: The Trinity and Christian Life.* New York: HarperCollins, 1991.

Lee, Bernard J. *The Galilean Jewishness of Jesus: Retrieving the Jewish Origins of Christianity.* Volume 1. *Conversation on the Road Not Taken.* New York/Mahwah, N.J.: Paulist Press/Stimulus Books, 1988.

———. *Jesus and the Metaphors of God: The Christs of the New Testament.* Volume 2. *Conversation on the Road Not Taken.* New York/Mahwah, N.J.: Paulist Press/Stimulus Books, 1993.

Martos, Joseph. *Doors to the Sacred: A Historical Introduction to Sacraments in the Catholic Church.* Exp. ed.; Tarrytown, N.Y.: Triumph Press, 1991.

McBrien, Richard P. *Catholicism.* 2 volumes. Minneapolis: Winston Press, 1980.

McGarry, Michael B. *Christology After Auschwitz.* New York/Ramsey, N.J./Toronto: Paulist Press, 1977.

———. "Roman Catholic Understandings of Mission." Martin A. Cohen and Helga Croner, eds. *Christian Mission—Jewish Mission.* New York/Ramsey, N.J.: Paulist Press/Stimulus Books, 1982: 119–46.

Meier, John P. *A Marginal Jew: Rethinking the Historical Jesus.* Volume 2. *Mentor, Message, and Miracles.* New York: Doubleday, 1994.

Meyer, Ben F. *The Aims of Jesus.* London: SCM Press, 1979.

O'Leary, Joseph Stephen. *Questioning Back: The Overcoming of Metaphysics in Christian Tradition.* Minneapolis/Chicago/New York: Winston Press, 1985.

Osten-Sacken, Peter von der. *Christian-Jewish Dialogue*. Margaret Kohl, trans. Philadelphia: Fortress Press, 1986.

Pawlikowski, John T. *Christ in the Light of the Christian-Jewish Dialogue*. New York/Ramsey, N.J.: Paulist Press/Stimulus Books, 1982.

———. *Jesus and the Theology of Israel*. Wilmington, Del.: Michael Glazier, 1989.

Perkins, Pheme. *Resurrection: New Testament Witness and Contemporary Reflection*. Garden City, N.Y.: Doubleday, 1984.

Sagan, Carl, and Ann Druyan. *Shadows of Forgotten Ancestors: A Search for Who We Are*. New York: Random House, 1992.

Sarna, Nahum M. *Genesis*. The JPS Torah Commentary. Philadelphia/New York/Jerusalem: Jewish Publication Society, 1989.

Schneiders, Sandra M. *The Revelatory Text: Interpreting the New Testament as Sacred Scripture*. San Francisco: Harper SanFrancisco, 1991.

Soggin, J. Alberto. *An Introduction to the History of Israel and Judah*. Valley Forge, Pa.: Trinity Press, 1993.

Soulen, R. Kendall. *The God of Israel and Christian Theology*. Minneapolis: Fortress Press, 1996.

———. "Removing Anti-Judaism." Howard Clark Kee and Irvin J. Borowsky, eds., *Removing Anti-Judaism from the New Testament*. Philadelphia: American Interfaith Institute/World Alliance, 1998: 149–56.

Speiser, E. A. *Genesis*. Anchor Bible Commentary. New York: Doubleday, 1964.

Therrien, Samuel. *The Elusive Presence: Toward a New Biblical Theology*. New York/Hagerstown, Md./San Francisco/London: Harper & Row, 1978.

Thoma, Clemens. *A Christian Theology of Judaism*. New York/Ramsey, N.J.: Paulist Press/Stimulus Books, 1980.

Trefil, James S. *The Moment of Creation: Big Bang Physics from Before the First Millisecond to the Present Universe*. New York: Charles Scribners' Sons, 1983.

van Beeck, Franz Josef. *Loving the Torah More Than God?—Toward a Catholic Appreciation of Judaism*. Chicago: Loyola University Press, 1989.

van Buren, Paul M. *A Theology of the Jewish-Christian Reality.* Vol. 1. *Discerning the Way* San Francisco: Harper & Row, 1980.

———. *A Theology of the Jewish-Christian Reality.* Vol. 2. *A Christian Theology of the People Israel.* San Francisco: Harper & Row, 1980.

———. *A Theology of the Jewish-Christian Reality.* Vol. 3. *Christ in Context.* San Francisco: Harper & Row, 1980.

Wilken, Robert L. *The Christians as the Romans Saw Them.* New Haven: Yale University Press, 1984.

———. *John Chrysostom and the Jews: Rhetoric and Reality in the Fourth Century.* Berkeley: University of California Press, 1983.

———. *Judaism and the Early Christian Mind: A Study of Cyril of Alexandria's Exegesis and Theology.* New Haven: Yale University Press, 1971.

Williamson, Clark M. *A Guest in the House of Israel: Post-Holocaust Church Theology.* Louisville: Westminster/John Knox Press, 1993.

Wilson, Marvin R. *Our Father Abraham: Jewish Roots of the Christian Faith.* Grand Rapids: Eerdmans/Dayton: Center for Judaic-Christian Studies, 1989.

Wright, N. T. "Adam, Israel, and the Messiah." *The Climax of the Covenant.* Minneapolis: Fortress Press, 1993.

Wyschogrod, Michael. *The Body of Faith: Judaism as Corporeal Election.* Minneapolis: Winston Press, 1983.

# Index of Documents Cited

*other volumes in this series*

*Stepping Stones to Further Jewish-Christian Relations: An Unabridged Collection of Christian Documents,* compiled by Helga Croner (A Stimulus Book, 1977).

Helga Croner and Leon Klenicki, editors, *Issues in the Jewish-Christian Dialogue: Jewish Perspectives on Covenant, Mission and Witness* (A Stimulus Book, 1979).

Clemens Thoma, *A Christian Theology of Judaism* (A Stimulus Book, 1980).

Helga Croner, Leon Klenicki and Lawrence Boadt, C.S.P., editors, *Biblical Studies: Meeting Ground of Jews and Christians* (A Stimulus Book, 1980).

Pawlikowski, John T., O.S.M., *Christ in the Light of the Christian-Jewish Dialogue* (A Stimulus Book, 1982).

Leon Klenicki and Gabe Huck, editors, *Spirituality and Prayer: Jewish and Christian Understandings* (A Stimulus Book, 1983).

Edward Flannery, *The Anguish of the Jews* (A Stimulus Book, 1985).

*More Stepping Stones to Jewish-Christian Relations: An Unabridged Collection of Christian Documents 1975–1983,* compiled by Helga Croner (A Stimulus Book, 1985).

Clemens Thoma and Michael Wyschogrod, editors, *Understanding Scripture: Explorations of Jewish and Christian Traditions of Interpretation* (A Stimulus Book, 1987).

Bernard J. Lee, S.M., *The Galilean Jewishness of Jesus* (A Stimulus Book, 1988).

Clemens Thoma and Michael Wyschogrod, editors, *Parable and Story in Judaism and Christianity* (A Stimulus Book, 1989).

Eugene J. Fisher and Leon Klenicki, editors, *In Our Time: The Flowering of Jewish-Catholic Dialogue* (A Stimulus Book, 1990).

Leon Klenicki, editor, *Toward A Theological Encounter* (A Stimulus Book, 1991).

David Burrell and Yehezkel Landau, editors, *Voices from Jerusalem* (A Stimulus Book, 1991).

John Rousmaniere, *A Bridge to Dialogue: The Story of Jewish-Christian Relations;* edited by James A. Carpenter and Leon Klenicki (A Stimulus Book, 1991).

Michael E. Lodahl, *Shekhinah/Spirit* (A Stimulus Book, 1992).

George M. Smiga, *Pain and Polemic: Anti-Judaism in the Gospels* (A Stimulus Book, 1992).

Eugene J. Fisher, editor, *Interwoven Destinies: Jews and Christians Through the Ages* (A Stimulus Book, 1993).

Anthony Kenny, *Catholics, Jews and the State of Israel* (A Stimulus Book, 1993).

Eugene J. Fisher, editor, *Visions of the Other: Jewish and Christian Theologians Assess the Dialogue* (A Stimulus Book, 1995).

Leon Klenicki and Geoffrey Wigoder, editors, *A Dictionary of the Jewish-Christian Dialogue* (Expanded Edition), (A Stimulus Book, 1995).

Philip A. Cunningham and Arthur F. Starr, eds., *Sharing Shalom: A Process for Local Interfaith Dialogue Between Christians and Jews* (A Stimulus Book, 1998).

Frank E. Eakin, Jr., *What Price Prejudice?: Christian Antisemitism in America* (A Stimulus Book, 1998).

Ekkehard Schuster & Reinhold Boschert-Kimmig, *Hope Against Hope: Johann Baptist Metz and Elie Wiesel Speak Out on the Holocaust* (A Stimulus Book, 1999).

Mary C. Boys, *Has God Only One Blessing?: Judaism as a Source of Christian Understanding* (A Stimulus Book, 2000).

Peter Wortsman, editor, *Recommendation Whether to Confiscate, Destroy and Burn All Jewish Books: A Classic Treatise against Anti-Semitism* by Johannes Reuchlin (A Stimulus Book, 2000).

Avery Dulles, S.J. and Leon Klenicki, editors, *The Holocaust, Never to Be Forgotten: Reflections on the Holy See's Document* We Remember (A Stimulus Book, 2000).

STIMULUS BOOKS are developed by Stimulus Foundation, a not-for-profit organization, and are published by Paulist Press. The Foundation wishes to further the publication of scholarly books on Jewish and Christian topics that are of importance to Judaism and Christianity.

Stimulus Foundation was established by an erstwhile refugee from Nazi Germany who intends to contribute with these publications to the improvement of communication between Jews and Christians.

Books for publication in this Series will be selected by a committee of the Foundation, and offers of manuscripts and works in progress should be addressed to:

Stimulus Foundation
c/o Paulist Press
997 Macarthur Boulevard
Mahwah, N.J. 07430
www.paulistpress.com